Money for Good Grades and Other Myths About Motivating Kids

In this helpful resource, expert educator Barbara R. Blackburn guides parents through the top eight myths about motivation and reveals what really works for kids. Each chapter is filled with practical information and stories that help you understand how to handle a variety of situations related to your child's success at school. Blackburn helps you get to the bottom of issues such as:

- Is motivating with rewards effective?
- What if your student doesn't care about school?
- How does your relationship with your student affect their motivation?
- How can you set high expectations without too much pressure?
- Is it okay for my kid to struggle, get stuck, and fail?
- How does competition affect success in school?
- What should you do when nothing seems to be working?

Chapters also include specific classroom connections for each strategy, so you can begin proactively working with your child's teacher. With the accessible advice in this book, you'll be able to reach your child more effectively so that he or she is more motivated from within, and more successful in school and beyond!

Bonus: Guides for collaboration between parents and schools are available on our website at www.routledge.com/9781138368200 so that schools can use the book to work more effectively with parents through PTA and PTO organizations, family support groups, and more. You'll also find a guide for parents to use to facilitate book clubs or reading groups.

Barbara R. Blackburn, Ph.D., a Top 30 Global Guru in Education, has taught early childhood, elementary, middle, and high school students and has served as an educational consultant for three publishing companies. In addition to speaking at conferences worldwide, she also regularly presents workshops for teachers and administrators. She is the author of more than 20 books, including the bestseller *Rigor Is Not a Four-Letter Word*.

Money for Good Grades and Other Myths About Motivating Kids

Strategies for Parents and Teachers

Barbara R. Blackburn

Routledge
Taylor & Francis Group

NEW YORK AND LONDON

First published 2019
by Routledge
52 Vanderbilt Avenue, New York, NY 10017

and by Routledge
2 Park Square, Milton Park, Abingdon, Oxon, OX14 4RN

*Routledge is an imprint of the Taylor & Francis Group,
an informa business*

Library of Congress Cataloging-in-Publication Data
A catalog record for this book has been requested

ISBN: 978-1-138-36819-4 (hbk)
ISBN: 978-1-138-36820-0 (pbk)
ISBN: 978-0-429-42938-5 (ebk)

Typeset in Palatino
by Apex CoVantage, LLC

Visit the eResources: www.routledge.com/9781138368200

MIX
Paper from
responsible sources
FSC
www.fsc.org   FSC™ C013985

Printed in the United Kingdom
by Henry Ling Limited

This book is dedicated to my parents.
They were, and still are, my inspiration in all areas of my life.

Contents

Meet the Author

A Top 30 Global Guru in Education, Dr. Barbara R. Blackburn has dedicated her life to raising the level of rigor and motivation for professional educators and students alike. What differentiates Barbara's 20-plus books are her easily executable concrete examples based on decades of experience as a teacher, professor, and consultant. Barbara's dedication to education was inspired in her early years by her parents. Her father's doctorate and lifetime career as a professor taught her the importance of professional training. Her mother's career as school secretary shaped Barbara's appreciation of the effort all staff play in the education of every student. Barbara has taught early childhood, elementary, middle, and high school students and has served as an educational consultant for three publishing companies. She holds a master's degree in school administration and was certified as a teacher and school principal in North Carolina. She received her Ph.D. in Curriculum and Teaching from the University of North Carolina at Greensboro. In 2006, she received the award for Outstanding Junior Professor at Winthrop University. She left her position at the University of North Carolina at Charlotte to write and speak full-time.

In addition to speaking at state, national, and international conferences, she also regularly presents workshops for teachers and administrators in elementary, middle, and high schools. Her workshops are lively and engaging and filled with practical information. Her most popular topics include the following:

- ♦ Rigor is NOT a Four-Letter Word
- ♦ Rigorous Schools and Classrooms: Leading the Way
- ♦ Rigorous Assessments
- ♦ Differentiating Instruction without Lessening Rigor in Your Classroom
- ♦ Motivation + Engagement + Rigor = Student Success
- ♦ Rigor for Students with Special Needs
- ♦ Motivating Struggling Students

Barbara can be reached through her websites www.motivatingyourkid.com and www.barbarablackburnonline.com

Acknowledgements

To my husband, Pete, who is the "wind beneath my wings," and my stepson, Hunter, who I love very much.

To my two sisters, Becky and Brenda, for their support.

Abbigail, a special thank you. You and I make an unstoppable team.

A special thanks to Lori Williams, who worked diligently and was invaluable as my research assistant.

To Lauren Davis, my editor, thank you for encouraging me to write for a new and different audience.

To Jessica Bennett and Susan Gorman—thanks for your suggestions, which helped me clarify and refine the content.

To Jo Griffin, thank you for a wonderful cover design.

To Autumn Spalding, my project manager, for providing a smooth production process. You are a joy to work with.

Finally, to everyone who is a parent or is connected to a kid: thank you for making a difference.

eResources

To enhance your reading experience and help you share your reading experience with others, I've provided two resources that are available online.

First, you'll find a **Guide for Book Clubs**, which was written in response to parents who requested ideas they could use to share with their neighbors and friends. It includes sample discussion questions and additional thoughts for reflection.

Next, there are guides for educators, which include a **Facilitator's Handbook for Parent-Teacher Book Groups**. Many of my former graduate students who are teachers have found that parent-teacher book clubs were a way to learn about a topic as well as strengthen the relationship between parents and teachers. In addition, both parents and teachers were able to better respond to kids' needs. In order to facilitate that process, I created a handbook that includes discussion questions and application activities. You'll also find other useful materials online.

Introduction

Are you a stressed-out parent? I am, as are most parents I know. We all deal with some level of stress, and much of that comes from our kids. As I was researching this book, I heard over and over again, "My son or daughter doesn't want to do his or her chores, follow directions, or finish his or her homework." Sometimes it seems as though our kids are not motivated to do anything we want them to do.

This book is designed to address that specific issue. We'll be looking at eight major myths of motivation, including that rewards are your best motivational tool, allowing your kid to fail many times is good for them, and competition is not a big deal. Each chapter is filled with practical information and stories that help you understand how to handle a variety of situations. Additionally, throughout the chapters, you'll find *Mixed Messages*, which are comments that may be misinterpreted by your son or daughter. Finally, at the end of each chapter there are *Classroom Connections* with suggestions for questions to ask your kid's teacher and ideas you might share with the teacher. If you are feeling particularly anxious, skip to Chapter 8, which deals with what to do when nothing works.

Before we jump into the myths, let's take a look at some basic information.

Extrinsic and Intrinsic Motivation

There are two main types of motivation: extrinsic and intrinsic. Extrinsic motivation includes all the outside ways we try to influence a student, such as rewards, prizes, or grades. Intrinsic motivation comes from within your son or daughter. With extrinsic rewards, we can get temporary results, but for long-term impact, we need to help students activate their intrinsic motivation.

Intrinsic motivation is that which comes from within your kid. It is internal as opposed to external. With intrinsic motivation, kids appreciate activities for the sake of those activities. They enjoy learning and the feelings of accomplishment that accompany the activity. There are many benefits to intrinsic motivation. Students tend to earn higher grades, score higher on achievement tests, prefer challenging activities, and are more confident about their abilities.

It's similar to looking at the ocean. I love watching the waves, but I'm only seeing the surface. I don't see the perilous undercurrents. Similarly, extrinsic motivation looks good, but we don't notice the dangers. Also, the true beauty of the ocean is underneath the surface. As we go deeper, there are beautiful marine creatures, fish, and coral. Instead of short-lived waves, I can see long-lasting beauty. And that is intrinsic motivation.

We'll take an in-depth look at extrinsic motivation in Chapter 1, then we'll move on to intrinsic motivation in Chapter 2. From there, we'll explore other aspects that impact your kid's motivation. As you read the book, please don't hesitate to contact me with questions. I love hearing from parents! You can reach me at bcgroup@gmail.com or through my website at www.motivatingyourkid.com. Enjoy your reading!

1

Myth One

Motivating With Rewards
Is the Best Option

One of the most common ways to motivate kids is to use rewards. In fact, you were probably rewarded when you were growing up. Rewards are woven throughout society in the form of shopping rewards, points for travel, and discounted admission to events. We reward our kids with things, such as money, toys, electronic downloads for music, movies, games, and books, or food treats. We also use the concept of time, providing extra time on the computer or television, or delaying bedtime or a curfew. Third, we reward through events, such as allowing kids to go to the movies, mall, library, restaurant, or a friend's house or apartment.

However, using rewards as a motivational tool is one of the biggest myths related to motivation. Despite their popularity, they are not as effective as we assume. In this chapter, we'll explore the benefits of rewards, the problems with rewards, how to use (and not use) rewards appropriately, the role of consequences and punishment in motivation, and the concept of praise.

Are there problems with rewards?
Why should I use rewards?
How can I effectively use rewards?
What about consequences and punishment?
Is praise good or bad?
What are the characteristics of effective praise?

Are There Problems With Rewards?

Despite their popularity, are there problems with rewards? Actually, yes. There are five negative aspects of rewards.

Rewards are temporary.
Rewards can change your relationship.
Rewards don't address underlying reasons, and are ineffective long term.
Rewards reduce intrinsic motivation.
Better to create creative way to do task.

First, rewards are temporary. They simply do not work on a long-term basis. When I was working on this book, I experienced writer's block, which rarely happens to me after 23 books. Despite encouragement from my family and friends, a change of scenery, various attempts at a different starting point, and other strategies, nothing worked. I finally jump-started my writing by identifying a reward I wanted that I would get after I wrote at least a half chapter. Once I started, I was able to move forward on my own without additional rewards. It reminded me of a fire. Once you get a starter log going, it fans the rest of the wood to start a fire. A note of caution, however: if you continue to use rewards, kids' expectations become bigger. For example, you may start with giving him or her $1 for an A. Over time, they want $5, then $10, and they never want it to stop.

Second, rewards can change your relationship with your kids. Rather than a loving and caring relationship, rewards sometimes create a power structure: you dominate your kids' behaviors by manipulating them with bribes. They jump through hoops for your approval via rewards, which send the message that they are not valued for who they are. Ultimately, the focus of your relationship is on compliance, which is facilitated by rewards and threats, and on monitoring your kids' behaviors.

Next, rewards do not address the underlying reasons for your kid's behavior, therefore, you don't solve the real problem. For example, if your teenager only cleans his or her room when a reward is provided, there is another issue. Sometimes teenagers simply don't care, others are rebelling against authority, and still others want to do what their friends are doing.

Rewards also undermine intrinsic motivation. We'll discuss aspects of intrinsic motivation in Chapter 2, but for now, it's important to know that intrinsic motivation comes from within your kid and is far more lasting than rewards. The more we reward a behavior, the more we shift a kid's motivation to something external, which takes the focus away from their internal motivation. One of my friends had a son who loved reading before he started school. He continued in the primary grades, becoming a voracious, enthusiastic reader. When he started 3rd grade, his teacher introduced a program to monitor and incentivize reading. Students read a book from an approved list and took a computer test. They earned points, and then prizes based on their reading. That sounds really great, doesn't it? For my friend's son, however, there was a different result. Many of the books he wanted to read were not on the approved list, or at the approved level, since he wanted to read more challenging books. Before long, he was reading less, and continually commented he had to read the "right books to earn points." Over time, his interest waned, and he saw reading as just another chore. It took several years for him to regain his love of reading.

Finally, it's simply more effective to find other, creative ways to encourage kids to engage in tasks. Ideally, your kids come up with these options on their own, rather than looking to you for ideas. This creates ownership and reinforces the notion that they have choices and control, even though they may be doing something required by an adult. I've seen kids sing or dance while vacuuming the house, find a practical reason for completing homework (such as using the information in college or in a job), or create a stronger bond with you or another family member by completing the task together. The goal is to help your kids find ways to motivate themselves internally, which we will explore in the next chapter.

Why Should I Use Rewards?

You may be thinking, based on the description of negative aspects of rewards, that you should never use rewards. Based on my experiences, I believe there are limited uses for it. For example, I agree with Daniel Pink (2011), author of *Drive*, who compares extrinsic motivation to caffeine, noting it gets you going (although you are less motivated later). There were times that the only way I could get myself, my stepson, or my nieces and nephews motivated was with a reward. It was effective, and oftentimes I could then move them beyond the initial reward.

Additionally, when there is no interest because a task simply is not enjoyable, such as cleaning a room or memorizing information or if there has been a history of misbehavior, it can be necessary to create an external reward as a jump start for good behavior. Daniel Pink also points out that extrinsic rewards do work for a short time for mechanical, rote tasks, so there are benefits to rewards in certain situations. This would be true at any age; you'll want to balance when you use an external reward.

Richard Ryan and Edward Deci (2017) help us understand rewards from a different perspective. They point out there are four basic purposes of rewards. First, we reward simply being present, such as eating dinner without the cell phone or attending a school event. Next, there are times we want to appreciate when our kids complete an activity, such as completing chores or homework. Third, we incentivize performance, which may be related to grades or an artistic endeavor. Finally, we celebrate times when students are winners, whether it is winning the science fair or a football game.

The clearest benefit of rewards is that it encourages and ensures compliance. Our kids are more likely to comply with our request or with a task if we reward them. But is it enough when our kids simply do what they are told? As J. Reeve (2014) points out, there are unintended consequences of rewards, which outweigh the limited benefits.

Unintentional effects.
Undermines intrinsic motivation.
Undermines ownership.
Undermines self-regulation.

Mixed Messages

Every night, when you finish your homework, you can earn credits for an online game.
(For kid who is interested in nature) I'll pay you to work in the yard.

This leads us to our next point: How can I effectively use rewards?

How Can I Effectively Use Rewards?

I'm often asked, "I'd like to continue using some rewards. Are there any positive ways to do that?" The simple answer is yes. Let's look at seven strategies that can help you use rewards effectively.

> Realize Rewards Don't Work
> Ease Into Changes
> Watch for Surprise Moments
> Adjust as Time Goes On
> Reduce Amount Over Time
> Decide to Focus on Behavior
> Stick with the Plan

Realize Rewards Don't Work

The first step to using rewards effectively is to recognize that they do not have a long-term impact. I would love to tell you that a bag of stickers, gift cards, and other rewards would help your kid grow into a motivated adult, but it simply isn't true. We must face the fact that rewards are easy and fun, but ineffective over time. This is the only way we can adjust to another approach toward motivation.

Ease Into Changes

I remember the moment when, as a teacher, I decided to move away from rewards. I was so committed to the concept of intrinsic motivation that I quit using them immediately, and never looked back. At some point, I realized that my students' motivations had dropped. Stopping cold turkey wasn't the best approach with them. I stepped back, explained what I would be doing with rewards moving forward, and shifted back to rewards, although at a lesser level. Over the next few weeks, I continued to reduce the frequency and amount of rewards, until my students were no longer reliant on them. You may choose to use some rewards, or no rewards. Whatever you decide, ease into it.

Watch for Surprise Moments

The most effective use of rewards is when they are a surprise. Randomly provide rewards at unexpected moments, and for unexpected things. For example, rather than giving your kid money when he or she earns an A on the report card, pick a time during the grading period and provide a reward for simply working hard.

Adjust as Time Goes On

As you transition through the process of motivating your kids, you will need to make some modifications. You may need to slow down or speed up the rate of reducing rewards. You also may need to increase or decrease the value of the reward, or change the type. Be flexible as you and your kids adjust to the changes.

Reduce Amount Over Time

As I just mentioned, you will want to make adjustments to your reward strategy. A key part of moving your kids away from a dependence on rewards is to reduce the rewards over time. I pointed out that you want to ease into the process of removing rewards, but ease implies forward movement. You may choose to reduce how often you provide rewards to your kids, which is definitely a positive step. You'll also want to reduce the value of the reward, whether or not it is monetary. Assess the rewards you are currently using, and determine ways to lessen the value. For example, if your kid expects $25 for every A on his or her report card, lower the amount. Or, if a reward for good behavior is a trip to the amusement park, find another experience that is not as complex.

Decide to Focus on Behavior

Many of those who research motivation advise that, when using rewards, you focus on specific behaviors, not the individual. Others feel that it is okay to reward someone just for being who they are. I tend to fall in the middle. Both have value, so it's important to consider why you want to reward your kid. If you believe he or she needs affirmation of who he or she is, then use a small reward that celebrates them personally. If your kid completes a task or is particularly successful with something challenging, you may want to surprise him or her with a reward for his or her work.

Stick with the Plan

Finally, stick with the plan you develop, whether it includes some rewards, or completely eliminates rewards. Make adjustments to individual aspects that you feel are appropriate, but stay on the path that reduces rewards. Your kids will complain and rebel, and other family members may beg you to change your mind and reinstate rewards again. Stay strong. Rewards lose their effectiveness over time, so don't give up when you meet resistance.

What About Consequences and Punishment?

How do consequences and punishment fit into our discussion of rewards? In many ways, they are the other side of the rewards coin. We give a reward, or we punish by taking something away, whether that is an object like a toy or phone or something that is time-related, such as an earlier curfew or sitting in time-out.

I was recently asked, "Are you saying I shouldn't ever punish my son? Sometimes he deserves it." I responded to the father that there are appropriate uses for punishment. However, we don't usually use punishment effectively. I've seen at least three problems related to punishment. First, too often, we threaten punishment, but don't follow through. When I was teaching, I remember one particular parent. She continuously threatened consequences if her daughter didn't "shape up and do your homework." He daughter never did her homework, and the parent never punished her. She learned that what her mother said didn't matter.

In another case, a friend of mine punished his child all the time. His daughter could make a minor mistake, such as forgetting to put her dishes in the dishwasher, and there was an immediate punishment. She learned that perfection was the only acceptable behavior. Finally, parents often use punishment that is either too harsh, or not strong enough. Two of my neighbors demonstrated this issue. One mother used severe punishments for minor mistakes. There was an instance where her daughter was grounded for a month when she only completed half of her homework one night. Another neighbor was more relaxed. When his son was caught shoplifting for the third time, he laughed it off, saying "He's just a kid. It's part of growing up." His wife insisted on a punishment, so he told his son he would need to give up his phone for two hours. These are two extremes of the concern—that punishment is often not appropriate.

Mixed Messages

I told you to clean your room! You are grounded for a month!!!
If you don't do your homework, you can't use your phone
[but you don't follow through].

There are parents who believe punishments and consequences are a useful strategy in a parenting toolkit. In *Ignore It! How Selectively Looking the Other Way Can Decrease Behavioral Problems and Increase Parental Satisfaction*, Catherine Pearlman (2017) points out that consequences can help kids learn what is considered an unwanted behavior. However, useful consequences are logical, reasonable, meaningful, and related to the unwanted behavior. If my teenager came home after curfew, and continued the behavior after a discussion and a warning, it would certainly be appropriate to move the curfew to an earlier time, or not allow my teen to go out one night.

Dr. Pearlman proposes a better solution to the issue of punishment and consequences. She suggests that natural consequences are a more effective deterrent to unwanted behavior than a superficial punishment. For example, suppose your middle schooler forgets his or her homework. There are two possible consequences. First, you can punish your kid by taking away his or her cell phone for a certain period of time, which may or may not change the behavior in the future. Or, you can sit back and let the natural consequence occur. In this case, your middle schooler would receive a zero for the assignment. One challenge with this approach is that some kids are not motivated by natural consequences. In this example, your middle schooler may not care if he or she receives a zero. In those specific cases, you may need to use external rewards and punishment. Keep in mind that you want to be cautious in terms of what, when, and how you use them.

She shares another example. A high school student who lives in Chicago leaves the apartment in January without a coat. After school, when he wants to attend an activity, he realizes how cold it is. Being so cold that he can't stay at the activity is a natural consequence that will serve as a reminder that he needs a coat in the winter. Natural consequences typically are more effective, and students are not manipulated into behavior through superficial punishments.

However, there is a roadblock to natural consequences: we "save" our kids from them. In the homework scenario above, many parents leave work to return home, pick up the homework, and take it to the school. This actually excuses the behavior we want to limit (forgetting homework). Similarly, we may rush to take our high schooler a coat, which does not allow for a natural consequence.

Natural Consequences

Natural Consequences	Our Actions That Prevent Natural Consequences
◆ A middle schooler decides to dye her hair blue without permission. She ends up with locks the color of seaweed. She hates it, classmates nickname her "Squid Girl," and she cries herself to sleep.	◆ A middle schooler decides to dye her hair blue without permission. She ends up with locks the color of seaweed. She hates it and runs crying to her parents. They are appalled and pay for the nearest salon to have it dyed back.
◆ Your kid waits until the last minute to complete a class project. When he turns it in, he gets a low grade, which means he doesn't make the honor roll.	◆ When you see the finished project after dinner, you realize he has done a bad job. You stay up late redoing it so he can make a good grade.
◆ A child protests at dinner because she says she hates vegetables. This is nonsense—she's eaten vegetables before. Mom says she will not have anything until breakfast. The child goes to bed hungry, and the rumbling of an empty stomach keeps her up at night.	◆ A child protests at dinner because she says she hates vegetables (even though she has eaten them before). She decides not to have dinner. But when she whines and moans later on, her folks decide that a small snack might be appropriate. She goes to bed with a full stomach, and she didn't have to eat the vegetables.
◆ A kid misbehaves during sports practice, and the coach doesn't start him or her in the game.	◆ You call the coach and convince him or her to reconsider, offering to provide volunteer help with a project that supports the sport.

Adapted from Pearlman, C. (2017). *Ignore It! How Selectively Looking the Other Way Can Decrease Behavioral Problems and Increase Parental Satisfaction*

As you can see, there is a clear contrast in natural consequences compared to parent-created punishment. Your kid learns about the ramifications of his or her behavior without the need for your interference. However, there are times that natural consequences should not be used. First, if someone else will have to deal with the natural consequences, you need to create one for your kid. For example, your kid might throw his older brother's phone in the toilet, and the phone cannot be repaired. The older brother would be subject to the natural consequences, so you will need to find alternative consequences for your kid, such as doing chores to earn money to help pay for a new phone.

Next, there are times that the natural outcome would be dangerous. If my nephew wanted to use matches, I can't risk letting the natural consequences play out. I wouldn't want him to be burned, and I can't afford for him to burn down the house. Finally, there are times that the natural consequence does not occur immediately. When there is a period of time between the action and the consequence, there is typically not a positive effect on the behavior. A high schooler taking a driver's education class may choose not to pay attention. The long-term effect is that he or she may end up in a wreck because he or she didn't focus in class. However, that is a long-term natural consequence that does not provide an immediate impetus for your high schooler to change his or her behavior.

Is Praise Good or Bad?

Parents, families, teachers, and other adults have mixed views on praise. We've all been recipients of praise, and that shapes our perspective. I have a friend who was always told, "Good job," "That's great," and "Awesome!" The praise was continual, so my friend took it for granted. It was also general, so he never knew what he was being praised for. I remember that my dad was less enthusiastic, reserving his praise for times I had accomplished something. He was also very specific as to what I did well (and what I did not!).

Richard Ryan and Edward Deci (1985a) explain that, in terms of motivation, it is not the praise itself, but how you share praise that makes a difference. Additionally, praise can balance criticism. Larry Ferlazzo describes a finding by A. McInnes, who notes that it takes three positive interactions for every critical one in order to develop and maintain a healthy team. The same applies to our kids. If they hear too many negative comments, it can be defeating and detrimental. For example, in school, students with special needs typically hear over eight negative comments for every one positive comment. These can come from other students, teachers, siblings, or parents. Add to this the fact that our brains are wired to remember negative things more than positive, and you have a kid who will struggle. So, there are benefits.

However, as with most things, there are also negative results of praise. Many of those who oppose rewards also oppose praise, saying that, with either one, you are manipulating kids. Consider that we praise or criticize to shape kids' behaviors and you can understand this perspective. As with rewards, you can create "praise junkies," kids who want more and more, and are unwilling to respond without the praise. Praise also shifts the focus from a kid's internal focus on interest and pleasure to an external focus that looks for affirmation and approval. Finally, there are some indications that praise can reduce achievement. We'll discuss this in the next section, but for now, just know that if we praise the wrong things, it can negatively affect your kids' learning. Ultimately, praise has mixed results.

What Are the Characteristics of Effective Praise?

How can I use praise in a manner that makes a difference with my kids? There are six key elements of effective praise.

Effective PRAISE

Positive
Real
Affirming
Independence is Promoted
Specific
Effort and Progress Are Noted

Positive

First, praise should always be positive. That may seem to be self-evident, but I've known parents who said they were praising their kids, but it was done in a sarcastic manner, with the corresponding body language. That undermines any positive effects of the praise. You may think sarcasm is an effective tool to use, particularly with older kids. I respectfully disagree. My experience is that, although kids don't show it, deep down, sarcasm reinforces any negative comments they've heard in the past. Again, too often, they experience enough sarcasm from their friends, siblings, other peers, or online. They need us to be encouraging. Here are three examples of negative praise, with the positive alternative.

Negative Praise	Positive Praise
Finally, you did it.	I knew you could do it!
Well, thanks for getting started [sarcastic tone].	That's a good start on your project.
Really, you finished your chores?	Your effort really paid off—you finished everything I asked you to do.

Real

Another important aspect of praise is that it is authentic. Kids are quick to recognize phony comments, and, when you make up praise, it undermines their trust in you. It's important to find real things you can authentically recognize in order to help your students build their motivation.

A. Faber and E. Mazlish, in their book *How to Talk so Kids Will Listen and Listen so Kids Will Talk*, give three suggestions that allow us to genuinely praise our kids. First, describe what you see. Rather than saying "Good job cleaning up the kitchen." say "I see that you put the dishes in the dishwasher, emptied the trash, and wiped down the countertops."

Next, you can describe how you feel. For example, you might say, "It's a pleasure to know that, since you have already finished your chores, we can spend some time together playing a game." Finally, a novel way to authentically praise your kids is to sum up the action with one word. "I notice that you finished your homework, organized them in your student agenda, and packed everything in your backpack so you are ready for school tomorrow. Now that is what I call *organized*!"

Affirming

Praise is also affirmation, which should be unconditional. In her book *Peaceful Parent, Happy Kids: How to Stop Yelling and Start Connecting*, Dr. Laura Markham addresses this issue, pointing out that unconditional affirmation is related specifically to your kid, which includes who he or she is and your love for him or her. In other words, move beyond praise that is conditional on actions.

How might this work? Laura also gives us some general types of praise that can help us understand this concept in a deeper way. You might empathize with her feelings by saying "It looks like you are enjoying that video game, it's the first thing you did after you finished your homework." Or, as we discussed earlier, comment on what your son is doing, which helps him feel noticed and valued. "When you are working on your project, I see that you are looking back at the instructions to make sure you are completing all parts of the project."

Next, you can communicate your enjoyment of sharing a task with your kid. For example, you could say, "I enjoyed cooking dinner with you. It's one of my favorite things we did today." You can also reflect how she feels about a task. Comments such as "It looks like you are really proud of finishing the project" echo their feelings rather than projecting your feelings onto her.

Finally, you can simply encourage your kid. Encouragement is totally unconditional, since it does not focus on successful completion of a task. I remember seeing a cartoon that exemplified this concept. There was a cartoon character who was fishing. He pulled out a huge fish, and there were comments from all bystanders. That's praise. The next character was also on the pier, but the fishhook was attached to the back of his pants. A friend said, "It's a little frustrating, isn't it. But you are almost there!" That is unconditional encouragement.

Independence Is Promoted

One thing that is particularly critical is that we use praise to empower our kids, rather than making them more dependent on us. Suggestions from Alfie Kohn, in *Unconditional Parenting:*

Moving from Rewards and Punishments to Love and Reason, helped me clarify ways we can encourage independence.

First, we can simply listen to our kids, and ask them how they feel. "What are they proud of?" Next, we can describe what we see, and ask them questions "What helped them be successful with the task?" Another option is to praise kids for how what they are doing affects others. "When you walked the dog tonight for your sister, how did that help her?" (that meant that, when she got home from work, she had time to study).

Notice that I have phrased the sample praises as questions rather than statements. By doing so, I am shifting ownership to my kid, and empowering him or her to be less dependent on external praise.

Specific

It's particularly important to be specific with our praise. Too often, we say "Good job" or "That's great." First, our kids don't really know what the praise is for. Second, it's so general, and so overused, that kids become numb to it. Be sure you praise very detailed items.

Examples of Specific Praise

I know you are proud of the A on your report card. What I noticed throughout the grading period was that you took notes in class and organized them, did your homework every day, and asked the teacher for help when you struggled on your tests. It's clear that's why you earned the A.

You did a good job cleaning your room by putting all your clothes in the closet and dresser and by making the bed.

I appreciate that you didn't come home after school and go outside to skateboard until you completed all your homework.

Effort and Progress Are Noted

Finally, effective praise focuses on effort and progress rather than ability. Carol Dweck, in her book *Mindset*, provides research that supports this concept. She found that if students are praised for their ability ("You're so smart"), over time, their effort and achievement decreases. But, if students are praised for their effort ("I can tell you tried hard and successfully read the paragraph"), over time their effort increases, as does their achievement.

When my stepson was in the 6th grade, he struggled with math. My husband was always telling him how smart he was, and that he could be successful. Then, one day, my husband heard me speak on this topic. He changed how he talked with Hunter, encouraging his efforts to learn the material. By the end of the year, Hunter was quite successful and scored above average on the achievement test.

Our kids do need to hear that they can learn and grow. But a part of that is encouraging them to try, and reinforcing that effort.

Sample Praise Statements That Reinforce Effort and Progress

Good, you noticed that mistake and fixed it.

I liked the way you tried to help yourself.

I can tell that you're really thinking about what you are doing.

I can see that you enjoy math. You have worked on these problems for over half an hour!

I really like how you used deductive reasoning to answer that question.

Mixed Messages

You **finally** did something right!

That was really great [in a sarcastic tone].

Summary

- ◆ Rewards are the most common way that kids are motivated.
- ◆ There are several negative aspects to using rewards.
- ◆ If you use rewards, do so sparingly and effectively.

- Natural consequences are more effective than parent-selected punishment over time.
- Praise can be an effective motivation tool if used appropriately.

Classroom Connection

Is there something I might ask my kid's teacher(s) about?

- How do you use rewards and other extrinsic motivators in your classroom?
- What is your approach to praise?

Are there any ideas I might share with my kid's teacher(s)?

- Your approach to extrinsic motivation with your son or daughter.
- Your alternatives to rewards and other extrinsic motivators.
- How you praise your kid.

2

Myth Two

What Your Child Cares About
Doesn't Matter

In the introduction, we discussed the difference between intrinsic, or internal, and extrinsic, or external motivation. Then, in Chapter 1, we took an in-depth look at extrinsic motivation. Here, we'll turn our attention to intrinsic motivation. Intrinsic motivation is that which comes from within your son or daughter. It is internal as opposed to external. With intrinsic motivation, students appreciate learning and other activities for their own sakes. They enjoy what they are doing; they are more engaged; and they are more creative. There are other benefits to intrinsic motivation. As students, they tend to earn higher grades, score higher on achievement tests, prefer challenging work, are more confident about their abilities, and retain information and concepts longer.

Why does intrinsic motivation, or what kids value, matter? See if you have ever experienced the following. "I am totally frustrated. It's like my son isn't interested in anything *I* think is important! My kid just isn't motivated!!" That's very common, but it's not what is actually happening. In reality, all kids are motivated, just not necessarily by what we want them to be motivated by. Our role is to tap into their existing internal motivation, and channel it in positive ways, which we can best accomplish by connecting with what he or she values. What our kids care about is the key to their motivation.

What Does Your Kid Value?

Although every kid is unique, we can consider how kids are motivated by discussing six types of value.

```
Basic Needs
Relationships
Interests
Activities
Competence
Autonomy
```

Basic Needs

Maslow's Hierarchy of Needs

In 1943, Abraham Maslow identified a hierarchy of needs that people experience.

```
Maslow's Hierarchy

Self-Actualization
Esteem
Love/Belonging
Safety
Physiological
```

He proposed that before one can focus on the need for esteem or self-actualization, which includes the need for knowledge or understanding, that the lower level needs, such as belonging, security, and survival, must be met. For example, from the very youngest age, if a kid's physical needs, such as adequate food, water, and shelter are not met, it's difficult for him or her to feel love or belonging. Maslow's work has continued to be relevant through the decades, because it is so accurate.

Applications of Maslow's Hierarchy

Needs Identified by Maslow	General Applications	Application to School and Learning
Self-Actualization (includes need for knowledge and understanding)	Am I able to pursue my own interests so I can learn and grow? Am I learning things that will help me be successful in life?	Focus on their own learning first. Will I have the knowledge to be successful?
Esteem Needs	Do I feel respected and valued by my family? Does my family encourage me and affirm my strengths?	Will I be successful? What will others think of me if I work hard?
Belonging Needs	Am I unconditionally loved and accepted by my family?	
Security Needs	Am I physically safe? Can I share my feelings safely?	What happens if I am unsuccessful?
Survival Needs	Am I well-nourished? Do I get enough sleep? Do I have safe shelter?	Do I have the knowledge and skills for success?

Relationships

Kids also value their relationships as another aspect of intrinsic motivation. Their relationship with you is so critical that we'll spend Chapter 3 addressing it, but there are other relationships they value. First, there are extended family members that make a difference in your son's or daughter's life. Although I have a very close relationship with my parents, one of my deepest family connections is with my grandmother. When I was growing up, I stayed with her and my grandfather every Friday night and Saturday. On Friday nights, she and I would talk and do craft activities, and on Saturdays I worked in the country store she and my grandfather owned. She took me on several trips and was

someone I could always talk to. I know she loved me uncondi-
tionally. Although she died over 25 years ago, I often think of her,
and when I'm discouraged, I remember the positive things she
said to me. Who in your extended family influences your son or
daughter? They play an important role in your kid's motivation.

Who else does your kid value? Usually there are other adults,
such as teachers, coaches, or neighbors that he or she is connected
with. Their opinions matter to your son or daughter, and they
can influence motivation. My neighbor's daughter is passionate
about math, in part because a female engineer at their church
noticed her interest and mentored her. Your kids also are influ-
enced by how they feel about their siblings, whether positive or
negative. Some kids try to imitate an older sibling; others rebel
against the comparison. You'll need to consider that dynamic as
it relates to your son or daughter's motivation. Finally, whether
we like it or not, our kids' peers make a difference. This can also
be good or bad, and although it is important when your kid is
younger, peers matter much more during the middle and high
school years. Several years ago, my niece became a cheerleader.
The impetus? Her best friend's participation in competitive
cheerleading. Notice that peer pressure can be extrinsic, since the
pressure comes from outside your son or daughter; but it is also
intrinsic because the value of connecting with peers is internal.

Mixed Messages

I know you are interested in art, but that's not really for boys.
I understand you like filming videos, but that career won't
  pay well.

Interests

Kids are certainly motivated by their internal interests. Teachers often talk about showing students the relevance or real-life
connections of a topic. When doing so, they are trying to tap into
their students' interests. It's important to consider that your kid's
interests may or may not match your own, and they may change

over time. For our part, we need to notice our kids' interests, support their interests if appropriate, and provide opportunities for them to pursue those interests.

Activities

Kids are also motivated intrinsically by different types of activities. Of course, activities that are related to relationships or interests are critical. For example, your daughter may want to attend a football game, not because she likes football, but because she wants to see her friends. Your son, on the other hand, may ask to attend a concert because he likes the artist's music.

Another aspect to consider is the type of activity your son or daughter prefers. Some kids are more social, and they learn and grow when they are with others. You've probably noticed teachers that incorporate groupwork or teaming in their instruction. They've found that many students learn more effectively when working with their classmates, and they capitalize on that to improve learning. You'll also want to consider that some kids are more introspective. Your son or daughter may prefer to explore their interests on his or her own. That is one style, and it is not necessarily better or worse than another style.

Other kids value physical activities. When my nephew was in kindergarten, he struggled learning words. My sister worked with him, trying to help him memorize the words and their meanings, writing out the words, and reading stories using the words. Nothing seemed to work. I had noticed that he was more engaged in his interests and other activities when he was physically involved in the tasks. I talked with him, and we created a game. He would go into the yard, draw the words in the sand, then draw an image that represented the meaning of the word. Together, we came up with other options, such as using playdough. It helped him connect with his learning.

Similarly, some kids are motivated by experiences. They want to visit a museum or go to work with an adult to learn about a topic. One of the positive aspects of technology is the ability for kids to explore places and topics virtually. If your young daughter is interested in animals, the San Diego Zoo provides a great virtual experience. And if your son who is in high school likes art, a virtual visit to the Louvre is a good opportunity. Again, some kids are different, and may prefer to learn about their interests in a more passive manner, such as reading about a topic.

Competence

Another aspect of value is competence, or success. When your son or daughter doesn't feel successful, he or she is more likely to give up or become disengaged. We will explore helping your kid face failure and overcome obstacles in Chapters 4 and 5, so we will look at major concepts here.

Recently, I read an advice column (www.washingtonpost.com/lifestyle/style/daughter-will-find-her-own-rhythm-even-if-rhythms-not-her-thing/2018/12/18/820ac56e-fff5-11e8-83c0-b06139e540e5_story.html) in which a parent had a common concern. Her daughter was very interested in becoming a member of the drill team at her high school, but coordination was not her strength. The mother wanted to know whether she should encourage or discourage the interest. The columnist's advice: ask neutral questions, offer options to help her daughter be successful, and love her for who she is. She also pointed out to the mother that it wasn't her job to tell her daughter she wouldn't be successful; that would be the coach's job. I agree. Our role is to be supportive and help kids develop competence. When competence meets interests, our kids develop passion, and isn't that our goal? Helping our kids find their passion in life?

Mixed Messages

Are you sure you want to play that sport? I'm not sure you are good enough.

I'm really not disappointed with that grade; I know you aren't very good in science.

Autonomy

Finally, kids value autonomy, or their independence. It's important for kids to see themselves as separate, responsible, competent people, and this is a core component of intrinsic motivation. This is a hard balance for parents. How much independence should we allow? I have struggled with that. How much is enough, while still providing some boundaries? Adele Faber and Elaine Mazlish, in their book *How to Talk So Kids Will Listen & Listen So Kids Will Talk*, provide a useful description of the process of encouraging autonomy.

> I know that for me the idea of encouraging the children to be in charge of the details of their own lives was revolutionary. I can still hear my grandmother saying admiringly of a neighbor, "She's the most wonderful mother. What she doesn't do for that child!" I grew up believing that good mothers "did" for their children. Only I took it one step further. I not only "did" for them, I thought for them as well. Result? Every day, over every trivial issue, there would be a contest of wills, ending with bad feelings all around. When I finally learned to turn over to the children the responsibilities that rightfully belong to them, everyone's disposition improved. Here's what helped me: Whenever I'd feel myself starting to get agitated or involved, I'd ask myself, "Do I have any choice here? . . . Must I take over? . . . Or can I put the children in charge instead?"

That's why it is so important to give our kids opportunities to be independent, whether it is picking out their own clothes for school, doing chores on their own, or finishing their own homework with minimal or no help. I'm not recommending you allow total freedom for your kids; I'm recommending that you help them develop their autonomy. In other words, you'll need to provide your son or daughter support as they are transitioning, and then lessen your support over time. For example, when I was a young girl, I wanted to ride a bike. However, I had to start with a tricycle. I needed to be close to the ground, and I needed the support of extra wheels. However, after a couple of years, I was ready to ride a children's bicycle. Of course, it had training wheels, because I still needed the balance of two additional wheels at the back. Next, I remember the day my father took off the training wheels so I could ride without them. He still held on to the back of the seat, to make sure I learned how to keep my balance without the extra wheels. Finally, he let go of the seat and let me ride by myself, one of the proudest days of my young life.

That's one way to think of helping your kids develop independence. Early on, kids may need strong, consistent support and boundaries so they don't falter. Then, lessen the support a bit, but still ensure that you have built-in assistance. Next, pull back a bit, but still stay close by to make sure they are successful. Lastly, they'll try things by themselves and thrive.

There is a strong reason to consider the process of developing autonomy, which starts at a young age. Many teachers talk about learned helplessness, which is when a student expects someone else to do his or her work or solve a problem. The students don't even try on their own; they have learned how to be helpless. I saw the beginnings of this with my neighbor across the street. She was in the yard with her two year old, throwing a ball back and forth. One time, he dropped the ball and it rolled about 10 yards away. She immediately ran over and brought the ball to him, rather than allowing him to get it himself. She was, unknowingly, teaching him to be helpless. For our kids to be successful in life, they need to learn to be confident in their own efforts. Helping them become independent is one way to build their motivation, and their life skills.

Mixed Messages

I know you could do this by yourself but let me help you! [In a conversation with a family member] My son likes to try things on his own, but I like to make sure he can do things as well as I can.

How Do I Connect With My Kid's Value to Impact Their Motivation?

Now that we understand the six aspects of value, let's discuss how to connect with your kid's value so you can help your son or daughter build his or her intrinsic motivation in a positive direction.

Basic Needs

In order to meet our kids' basic needs, we should take what we learned and take actions to meet those needs. Remember that our goal is for our kids to reach self-actualization, and, in order to do so, the lower level needs must be met.

Needs Identified by Maslow	What We Can Do
Self-Actualization (includes need for knowledge and understanding)	Provide opportunities for your son or daughter to learn and grow. Help them explore their interests, encourage creativity, and dream! Work with them to build on their strengths, so they can reach their full potential.
Esteem Needs	Affirm your kids' strengths and reinforce their efforts to learn and grow. Respect what your kids do, but also who they are. Don't compare them to others. Ask questions about their feelings about successes and challenges and help them process how to deal with challenges.
Belonging Needs	Regularly reinforce that you love your son or daughter unconditionally, and that he or she will always be your kid, no matter what. Include your kid in your life. Schedule regular time with your kid.
Security Needs	Ensure your kids' physical safety, which includes making sure they feel safe going to and from school and other places. Address any bullying issues. When your son or daughter talks to you, be non-judgmental. Facilitate a positive relationship with your kid's teacher(s) and other adults.
Survival Needs	Provide adequate portions of healthy food to meet your kid's nutritional needs. This may mean adjusting meals or the types of snacks in your home. Focus on water as the primary form of liquid nourishment. Be sure your son or daughter gets enough sleep each night. This may be a challenge given school schedules and pick-up times for the school bus, but adjust bedtimes and curfews to ensure adequate rest. Provide a space your son or daughter can call "home." Whether you live in a mansion, with relatives, or in a shelter, add small touches that help your kids understand it is a safe place. These might include a designated family room, a quiet space in a relative's house or apartment, or taping a picture on the wall in a shelter.

Relationships

As I said earlier, we'll address how to build a motivating relationship with your kid in the next chapter. For now, keep in mind that your relationship with your son or daughter outweighs almost everything else. If he or she has a positive relationship with you, he or she will be more open to speaking with you and listening to you, and he or she is more likely to respond to situations in a productive manner.

Interests

How can we respond to our kid's interests? First, we need to take notice of his or her interests, which may require a bit of detective skills. Paying attention and asking questions are two effective tools. For example, you may think all your kid wants to do is watch TV or YouTube videos. However, with further investigation, you discover that he or she is interested in shows or video clips focused on science. Then, you are able to talk with your son or daughter and help him or her explore his or her interest on a deeper level. You can also learn about his or her interest, ask him or her to help you understand the topic or activity, and connect with him or her more closely. A quick caution: unless it is dangerous, don't dismiss or belittle his or her interest. We need to preserve our relationship, and if we want our kids to be motivated and successful, we should honor their perspective.

Questions to Gauge Interest

What do you like to read/talk/think about?
What is your favorite subject at school?
If you could watch any TV show, what would it be?
What games do you like to play on the tablet?
What is/are your favorite video game(s)?
What do you and your friends have in common?
If you could do anything for your birthday, what would it be?
If you could take a trip, where would you go?

Activities

In order to connect with the type(s) of activities your kids prefer and motivate them, we need to find out what they like and how they like to learn and grow. You can determine this through your own observations, by asking your son or daughter, gathering input from his or her teacher or other adults, or using a simple personality test. Two quick online quizzes are 365 Tests (https://365tests.com/personality-tests/what-type-is-your-child/) and a Meyers-Brigg test for kids (www.personalitypage. com/cgi-local/build_pqk.cgi). Be sure to check the privacy settings, or you may simply choose to use the questions to guide a discussion.

Next, find opportunities that match your kid's preferred style. If he or she is extroverted and likes to be around others, provide times he or she can complete homework with a classmate, visit the library or a museum with friends, or share what he or she is learning with others. If he or she is more introspective, create a private space for alone time. If you ask a question, give him or her time to process before jumping in with your own answer. Or, offer your son or daughter a journal, where he or she can write about his or her feelings, experiences, or learning. If so, allow your kid to keep it private; no peeking!

If your son or daughter prefers kinesthetic, or physical activities, keep plenty of supplies that allow him or her to manipulate items related to his or her interests and concepts he or she is learning in school. My niece is interested in coding, and she prefers to create a code using an app on her tablet as opposed to listening to a teacher explain the purpose and steps. In today's world, computer apps do provide an interactive activity that is kinesthetic on some level. Moving around frequently, creating gestures to demonstrate concepts, and building models are other options.

For kids who are motivated by experience, plan for day trips, visits to libraries, museums, parks, and zoos. This may be expensive, or you may live in an area with limited options. As I mentioned earlier, virtual experiences, whether online or through virtual reality games, are a reasonable option.

Sample Virtual Experiences

San Diego Zoo: https://kids.sandiegozoo.org

A Variety of Virtual Farms: www.farmfood360.ca/?utm_source=domain&utm_campaign=www.virtualfarmtours.ca&utm_medium=redirect

Monterey Bay Aquarium: www.montereybayaquarium.org/animals-and-exhibits/live-web-cams

Smithsonian Museum of African American History and Culture: www.smithsonianmag.com/smithsonian-institution/national-museum-african-american-history-and-culture-interactive-museum-tour/

Smithsonian Postal Museum: https://postalmuseum.si.edu/visit/virtual-tour.html

Smithsonian National Museum of Natural History: www.visualconstruction.com/SI/index.html

360 Degree Tour of a Marine Exploration Vessel: www.marine.ie/Home/sites/default/files/VirtualTour/index.htm

Pacific Northwest National Labs (math): www.pnnl.gov/about/tour.asp

Louvre: www.louvre.fr/en/visites-en-ligne

A Variety of Tours Related to Music: http://collections.nmmusd.org/galleries.html

Denali National Park, Alaska: www.nps.gov/dena/learn/photosmultimedia/index.htm

A Variety of Tours from the National Park Service: www.nps.gov/museum/

Finally, for more passive learners who want to read about topics, provide opportunities for your kids to find books, whether that is visiting the public or school library, buying books for their own collections (yard and garage sales are a great budget-friendly source), or looking for free or paid books online. Keep in mind that articles, websites, newspapers, blogs, comic books, and graphic novels are also helpful.

Mixed Messages

Tell me about what you like [and then you check email during the conversation].

[After they tell you what they like] I'm glad you are interested in that, but let's focus on other things.

Competence

How can we help our kids build their intrinsic motivation through their success, or how can they demonstrate competence in their lives? As I mentioned earlier in this chapter, that answer requires far more depth than we can address here. In Chapter 4, we'll look at how to redefine failure and look at those disappointments in a different way. We'll also discuss building a growth mindset, grit, and perseverance. Then, in Chapter 5, we'll turn our attention to strategies that can help your son or daughter get "unstuck."

Autonomy

Autonomy, or the level of self-directedness of your kids, is very important to their motivation. Not only does it increase their intrinsic motivation, autonomy is a necessary life skill. There are a variety of ways to help our kids become autonomous and independent, but it starts with our commitment to help them do so. When I was a university professor, I encountered "helicopter parents," those who are always hovering about their kids, waiting to solve their problems. We'll talk more about this is Chapter 4, but let me share a brief example related to autonomy. I'll never forget a meeting in which a 22-year-old senior who was about to graduate brought his mother with him. She was not happy that, because of one grade in one course, he would not wear an honor cord over his graduation robe. Quite agitated, she spent over 45 minutes explaining in great detail how hard he had worked, how unfair the grade was, and how this would ruin his life.

On the other hand, he looked at the floor the whole time, and never spoke. He was clearly embarrassed, and he later told me he did not ask her to come, nor was he concerned about the honor cord. It was more about her, and her goals, not his, and she was determined to "fix it" since he wouldn't (or perhaps couldn't). Is that what you want for your son or daughter? I know I don't. I want my stepson and my nieces and nephews to grow up to handle their own problems. One time, my dad told me that the purpose of education was to teach students to learn what to do when they didn't know what to do. I think that's also one of the purposes of our motivating and parenting our kids. There are four ways you can help your kids become more independent.

Helping Your Kid Become Independent

Provide opportunities for them to make their own choices (perhaps with limited guidelines from you), whether it is what they wear to school, which extracurricular activity they prefer, or where they want to work part-time.

Respect them when they struggle. Rather than solving their problems, help them think about a situation, as well as possible solutions so they may determine the best option. Ask questions, rather than telling them what to do.

Encourage them when they want to try something on their own, rather than trying to prevent them from failing. This can range from a young child trying to help you clean up the kitchen, or your middle or high schooler wanting to take a more advanced class. Failure is a natural part of life, and our role is to encourage, support, and possibly comfort them.

Step back a bit and adjust your approach as your son or daughter grows older. This can be difficult, because we want to protect our kids. But the way we learned to be independent was through a series of opportunities. Also, being autonomous is foundational to our motivation. Let them try on their own, even if you have to bite your tongue and sit on your hands.

Summary

- Intrinsic motivation comes from within your kid.
- Intrinsic motivation is based on what your son or daughter values.
- Kids need to have their basic needs met in order to thrive.
- Find out your son's or daughter's interests and provide opportunities for them to tap into them.
- Kids need autonomy; allow them to be independent and make choices.

Classroom Connection

Is there something I might ask my kid's teacher(s) about?

- Do you think my son or daughter is intrinsically motivated? If so, how do you know?
- How do you encourage intrinsic motivation in your classroom?

Are there any ideas I might share with my kid's teacher(s)?

- Your kid's interests and what he or she values.
- The types of activities he or she prefers.

3

Myth Three

It's Not About Your Relationship With Your Kids

Many years ago, my father was on a flight from Washington, D.C., to New Orleans. He struck up a conversation with the gentleman next to him. At one point in the discussion, my dad asked, "What is the one thing you have learned in life?" The man responded, "I've learned that men can get along with other men if they try." At the end of the flight, he introduced himself— Martin Luther King, Sr. What a powerful statement. We can get along if we try, and sometimes we have to try for a long time. This is especially true with our kids.

Why Is Your Relationship With Your Kid So Important?

You might wonder why I would dedicate an entire chapter to the idea of building a relationship with your son or daughter, especially if you already have a strong connection with your kid. I do so because it is such an important concept in terms of motivation for your son or daughter. In Chapter 2, we discussed the link between what kids value and their level of intrinsic motivation. One of the types of value is the relationships they have with their parents, extended family, peers, and other adults.

Your relationship with your kid affects all interactions between you. If you have a good relationship with your son or daughter, he or she will be more motivated to listen your input, he or she will learn how to have positive relationships with others, and he or she is more likely to be successful in life. If you have a less constructive relationship, it is very difficult to connect positively with him or her and help develop his or her motivation.

When I was writing this chapter, I asked my sister for her perspective on relationships between parents and kids. She is the mother of a 12 year old who has just started middle school. As she related, "trust is the center of all relationships, not just kids. If she trusts me, when she's hurting, she'll talk to me rather than keeping things from me, so I can help her. I fear the things I see happening when kids didn't trust their parents enough just to talk to them. So many times, kids are involved with drugs or commit suicide, and they say that 'I had no one to talk to.'"

My husband has a similar perspective. He believes that relationships drive everything that happens between you and your kid, and that they are more important than many other issues. He points out, "grades last a semester; relationships last a lifetime."

How Can I Better Connect With My Kids?

One of the most common questions I hear from parents is "How can I better connect with my kid?" Marcia Tate (2011) describes the concept of the emotional bank account. When you make deposits of honesty, kindness, respect, courtesy, and other positive actions, your kid ends up with a large bank account. Then, when you respond to a situation in a less than positive manner, the amount of trust that you have built with your son or daughter balances your mistakes.

Three Ways to Connect With Your Kids

Model Who You Want Your Kid to Be
Relate in a Way that Matches Your Kid's Personality
Create an Environment that Supports Your Relationship

Model Who You Want Your Kid to Be

If you want to build a strong relationship with your son or daughter, you'll need to pay attention to your actions. You are a role model for your kids, whether you want to be or not. Michael Mendizza and Joseph Chilton Pearce, in their book *Magical Parent, Magical Child*, point out that according to a variety of studies, only 5% of lifelong learning comes from instruction; the other 95% of what we remember comes from family and social interactions.

Although we'll be discussing the importance of our language later in this chapter, our actions are more important than our words. The old adage, actions speak louder than words, is very true. From the youngest age, our kids pay attention to what they see, and their beliefs and own behaviors are shaped by what we do. There are three keys to modeling who you want your kid to be: model authenticity, be honest, and match your words and your actions.

Mixed Messages

I'm here when you need me, but you know there are times I'll need to do something else.

I'm listening [when your eyes are darting back and forth to your phone].

Relate in a Way That Matches Your Kid's Personality

Mary Sheedy Kurcinka, in her book *Raising Your Spirited Child*, describes a variety of personality types related to, but not limited to, spirited kids. It is helpful to consider these categories as we work to build our relationship with our kids.

Personality Type	Characteristics	How to Connect
Introverts	Rejuvenate while alone or with one or two close friends or family members; refresh with quiet time; need their own time to interact positively with others.	Recognize they need their own time and provide opportunities and space for them to be alone. Allow them time to reflect before responding to you.

(Continued)

(Continued)

Personality Type	Characteristics	How to Connect
Extroverts	Draw energy from others and engaging in the world around them. Enjoy interacting with others.	Provide opportunities to be around others. Talk to them to help them think through problems.
Intense Kids	Have intense emotions; are spirited, and are often scared and upset.	Keep calm; reassure them, remind them of the positive aspects of their personality.
Perceptive Kids	Have keen senses but have problems with sensory overload. When that happens, they can become distracted or confused, and have problems focusing.	Remind them of the positive aspects of their personality; communicate in a variety of ways including writing or drawing; focus on what they can do; don't add to distractions; remember they notice more than other kids, so they will notice anything you are hiding.
Persistent Kids	Push and demand, even when others don't. May be too focused on their own perspective.	Remind them of the positive aspects of their personality; focus on understanding why an issue is important to your kid; focus on working together to solve problems.
Sensitive Kids	Feel emotions and are very sensitive to sounds, smells, sounds, and touch; can be overwhelmed by stimulation.	Remind them of the positive aspects of their personality; discuss their emotions and the sensations around them; be sensitive to overstimulation and try to protect them from it, including limiting time on electronics.
Irregular Kids	Are unpredictable and do not seem to fall into natural rhythms, such as sleep and hunger.	Remind them of the positive aspects of their personality; provide consistent routines and a schedule; allow your son or daughter time to adapt to routines.

Understanding your kid's specific personality type and using that information to adjust your words and actions can help you build a stronger relationship with your son or daughter. Consider not only their personality type, but yours, and you'll connect on a deeper level.

Create an Environment That Supports Your Relationship

Kids also need an environment that supports your relationship. Consider the physical environment of your home. Does your kid have his or her own space when he or she needs time alone? Is there an area where family members can naturally spend time together? Next, think about the emotional environment. Is honest communication encouraged? Is conflict handled in a productive manner? Finally, reflect on the family's schedule. Is the calendar full, or is there regular time to connect? Are there opportunities for one-on-one time? Each of these areas help you create an environment that facilitates a close relationship with your son or daughter.

Assess the Motivation Level of Your Environment

Physical Environment	
Where does my kid have his or her own personal space?	
Where can my kid spend time with other family members?	
Emotional Environment	
How do you encourage open communication?	
What specific actions do you take to make sure conflict is handled in a positive manner?	
Scheduling Environment	
How is family time built into your calendar?	
When do you have regularly scheduled one on one time with each of your kids?	

Mixed Messages

"I'll respect your privacy" [then you enter their bedroom without knocking].

"I'll spend time with you" [but your schedule is full].

Does My Parenting Style Matter?

Our parenting styles shape our relationship with our son or daughter, as well as his or her level of motivation. Four parenting styles are commonly discussed: authoritarian, authoritative, permissive, and uninvolved. Let's look at Amy Morin's description (www.verywellfamily.com/types-of-parenting-styles-1095045) of the characteristics and implications of each, keeping in mind that most parents have a dominant style, but shift into other styles depending on the situation.

First, some parents are authoritarian. They believe they always know what is best; they are strict and controlling and they focus on punishment to force obedience. Kids who are raised by authoritarian parents may have lower self-esteem, often become angry or hostile, and may lie to avoid punishment.

Next, parents may take an authoritative stance, which blends love and caring with appropriate limits. They try to prevent problems, and take a positive approach to discipline. Their kids are most likely to become responsible adults who are confident and are comfortable expressing how they feel.

Third, some parents are permissive. Because they don't want to upset their kids, they allow their sons and daughters to do almost anything they want. Kids of permissive parents are more likely to struggle academically and may have low self-esteem. They often exhibit behavior problems, since they believe the rules do not apply to them.

Finally, there are uninvolved parents, who expect their kids to raise themselves. Sometimes, these parents have problems, such as drug use or mental health issues. Kids who are raised by uninvolved parents often struggle with self-esteem, are unhappy, act out behaviorally, and perform poorly in school.

I am biased on parenting styles. My parents were authoritative, and I believe that, overall, it is the most effective way to motivate your kids and help them become successful adults. No matter how you parent, if you want to motivate your son or daughter, incorporate respect and collaboration into your style. Show respect for your kid's emotions, perspective, and interests. When possible, collaborate to solve problems, rather than dictating a solution. Finally, be careful of how often you use the words "but" and "should," which can undermine your relationship.

How Can We Communicate More Effectively?

Commit to Open Communication
Open Your Ears
Maximize a Positive Approach
Minimize Confrontation
Understand the Hidden Signals
Nudge the Conversation in a Positive Direction
Indicate Your Support
Clarify When You Don't Understand
Ask Lots of Questions
Take a Risk
Encourage Further Communication

Commit to Open Communication

The foundational element of effective communication that motivates your son or daughter is that parents commit to open, two-way communication. We'll discuss specific strategies in the following sections, but if you aren't dedicated to being open to your kid's perspective, whether you agree with it or not, your kid will not be motivated to talk with you. It's not enough to say you are committed to open communication, your actions should reflect that commitment. First, be consistent and honor your word. Mixed messages can make your kids feel unsure and anxious, which undermines communication. If they aren't sure what you are going to say, they are less likely to talk with you. Second, be consistent with other parents and family members too. This can be particularly challenging in a divorce and/or remarriage situation. With multiple people who may have conflicting points of view involved, communication among adults is of paramount importance. When I was dating my husband, I was impressed that he and Hunter's mother worked to communicate about parental issues. He put forth a great deal of effort to make sure they were on the same page to ensure stability for Hunter.

Open Your Ears

One of the hardest parts of communication is listening. It's much easier to talk, since we want to share our perspective. When I was a teacher, I posted a sign on my wall that said, "Nature gave us two ears and one mouth so we could listen twice as much as we speak." That's a great guideline when we need to communicate with our kids. No matter the age, they need to be heard, which, in their minds, is a reflection of our respect for them. Although true for all kids, it's especially important for young adolescents and adolescents, who are reluctant to share. If they believe we aren't listening to them, they will withdraw from communication.

Listening is more than asking a question. I remember a friend's teenager telling her, "You say you are listening to me but you're not. There is a difference in hearing my words and listening to what I mean." How can you tell if you (or your kid) is truly listening?

Listening Indicators

When You and/or Your Kid is Listening	When You and/or Your Kid is Not Listening
Makes Eye Contact	Doesn't Look at the Other Person
Isn't/Aren't Doing Something Else (such as looking at phone)	Is Doing Something Else
Responds Appropriately to Questions or Comments	Doesn't Respond When a Question is Asked or Responds is a Way that Indicates a Lack of Attention
Nods or Makes Affirming Sounds	Makes Sounds that Reflect Disgust
Body Language is Positive (leaning toward other person, arms relaxed, smiling or neutral face, posture relaxes over course of conversation)	Body Language is Negative (arms folded, leaning back, angry face, glazed eyes, rolls eyes, stiff posture, shakes head consistently)

Maximize a Positive Approach

Every time you communicate with your kid, focus on the positive. This is particularly challenging when he or she is telling you something you don't like, or when you need to discuss a tough issue. It's easy to be positive when your son is sharing a success, but when your daughter is telling you about her first boyfriend (and you think she's too young to have a boyfriend), it's harder.

There are three ways you can maximize a positive approach with your kids. First, recognize that if your son or daughter is talking with you, it means he or she trusts you, which is important. Next, if your initial response is negative, take a deep breath before you say anything. Third, say something positive, even if you don't feel like it. For example, you might say, "I appreciate you sharing that with me. It's important that you felt you could tell me." Fourth, ask neutral questions that elicit information. Finally, if you have a way to affirm what he or she is telling you, do so. If you disagree or have another negative response, phrase it in a non-confrontational manner.

I saw one instance where a 10 year old admitted to his mom that he had broken his sister's toy and had lied about it. Naturally, his mom was frustrated, especially about the lying. She waited a few seconds, then commended him for telling the truth. Then, she asked why he waited, and he explained he was afraid she wouldn't love him anymore. She immediately hugged him and told him how much she loved him, and then explained why it was important to tell the truth. She finished by explaining that he would need to use his allowance to replace his sister's toy, and that he would be in time-out for lying, but that she was doing those things because she loved him, not because she didn't. She followed the process I described, and it was effective.

Mixed Messages

"Wow, you made a great point" [but in a sarcastic tone].
"I love you, as long as you don't lie to me again."

Minimize Confrontation

Part of promoting positive communication is minimizing confrontation. In some instances, this won't be an issue. But there are times, especially when the topic of communication is related to a disagreement between you and your kid, that you'll want to be mindful of addressing the situation without being confrontational. As a side note, there is a difference between confronting a situation and being confrontational. You can tackle a tough issue in a way that does not attack your kid. Let's look at three ways to avoid the negative aspects of confrontation.

First, watch your language. Particularly when we are trying to work through a challenging issue with our kids, our frustration can come out in words that may be harsh, and therefore unproductive.

Examples of Harsh Language	Examples of Softer Language
You must . . . Or else . . . My way is the only way . . .	How are we going to . . . Unfortunately, if we don't . . . , then . . . My perspective is valid, so let's find a way to make it work . . .
You are (fill in negative emotion, characteristic, or behavior) . . .	You are acting. . . . We both know that's not who you are.

Notice that in the softer language we shift from "You" and "Me" to "We." By doing so, our message becomes, "Yes there is a problem, but, together, we can find a solution." We can adjust our words so that we can move forward in a productive manner. You might consider avoiding words that are perceived as labeling, judging, or blaming.

Next, we should watch our tone of voice. Even if we use softer language, if we make a statement or ask a question in an accusatory or angry tone, our kids tend to shut down. Remember, relationship is important, and our tone of voice sends a loud message as to whether or not we value our kids

Finally, we need to watch our actions. I remember a parent conference I participated in when I was a teacher. My student had begun to exhibit some behavior problems, so I asked her parents to come in for a meeting. Her mother and uncle attended, and once I had explained what was happening, her uncle exploded. He stood up, towered over her, and started pointing his finger in her face. Of course, his words and tone of voice were also quite negative. My student put her head on the desk and started crying. Even though her mother comforted her and told her everyone loved her and wanted to help her, the uncle's behavior belied that. Needless to say, it was a totally unproductive meeting with no positive results.

Understand the Hidden Signals

There are two levels of communication: the seen, and the messages that are under the surface. It's easy to understand the surface level of communication, but in every instance, there are hidden signals and messages. We should always consider how our kids are feeling, not just what they are saying. Look at the following conversation with a Durrell, a middle schooler.

Dad, I don't want to do my homework. *Why not?* I just don't want to. It's dumb. *It doesn't matter. School is important, so do your homework.*

The overall message is clear. Durrell doesn't want to do his homework. And he gives a common excuse, "I don't want to. It's dumb." As we examine his explanation, we notice that he doesn't think homework is important. That goes back to one aspect of intrinsic motivation: value. Apparently Durrell doesn't see value in homework. However, as his father considers the situation, he realizes this isn't normal. Durrell usually does his homework, therefore, there is something else going on. There's a hidden reason he doesn't want to do his homework.

As the father asks questions and explores further, he discovers that the homework is for his science class. Durrell has been making As in science, and in the past few days, a couple of other students have been teasing him, calling him names and accusing him of being the teacher's pet. The real reason he doesn't want to do his homework is because he wants to fit in with his peers. Simply making Durrell do his homework doesn't solve the problem.

This situation requires Dad to work with Durrell over time to resist peer pressure.

Nudge the Conversation in a Positive Direction

We've discussed the need to be positive while communicating with your son or daughter, but there are times when a conversation turns negative. This can happen with your kid when he or she is frustrated or angry. When talking to her grandmother about a problem with a neighborhood friend, Malia began to list everything she "hated" about Bella. She was so upset that Bella had played with another neighbor, she forgot all the reasons she liked Bella. The more she talked, the more agitated she became. One small incident snowballed into a major problem. Her grandmother allowed her to talk for a bit, but then she started asking questions. "Why are you friends with Bella?" "Didn't you say you enjoyed playing with her yesterday?" "You said you were looking forward to her spending the night here this weekend. Why?"

As Bella began to respond to her grandmother's questions, it shifted her focus from the negative to the positive. Her grandmother continued to guide the conversation, resulting in Bella admitting she was jealous of the other girl, but that she knew Bella was still her friend. Later that afternoon, she apologized to Bella; all three girls played together, and the situation was over. In this case, shifting the conversation in a constructive direction resulted in a positive outcome. Crisis averted!

Indicate Your Support

We've already addressed that effective communication that motivates your kids is positive. A critical aspect of positive communication is the support you provide to your son or daughter. It doesn't matter how young or old your kid is, he or she needs to know that, no matter what, you will be there to support him. A close friend's son became involved in drugs. Although Mason said he wanted to stop, he was more motivated by the feelings generated by the drugs, and he struggled. One night, Mason overdosed and was taken to the emergency room. While his father raced to the hospital, he questioned why this had happened. Why hadn't he seen the signs? Why hadn't Mason told him? When he was able to talk with his son, Mason told him, through tears, that he was afraid his dad wouldn't love him anymore once he knew about the drugs. The father immediately reinforced his unconditional love and his unwavering support. Then, in the weeks and months following the conversation, the father showed his support by helping Mason set limits, stay out of negative situations, listening whenever Mason wanted to talk, asking questions when Mason became withdrawn, and assuring Mason that, if he found himself in a bad situation, he was to call his dad to pick him up, and that dad would not be judgmental about the mistake. Although it was a long road to recovery, which is still an ongoing battle, his dad's support helps him deal with the challenge.

Mixed Messages

"I know you made a mistake, and I love you enough to tell you never to make them again."

"I support what you are doing" [but then your son or daughter overhears you telling your spouse that you don't support them].

Clarify Everything

One of the hindrances to clear communication is when we make assumptions. We think we know what the other person said, but he or she is thinking something else. I remember asking my stepson to do a chore, and he responded "Uh-huh": 30 minutes later, I reminded him, and he again said "Uh-huh." Another 30 minutes passed, and, in a frustrated voice, I said, "You told me you would do the chore! I mean NOW!!!" He jumped up from the couch, looked at me, and replied, "I never told you I would do that." Talk about an assumption. His "Uh-huh" was not the "Yes, I will," I heard, it was just a sound so that I would let him play his video game. In retrospect, I should have asked him to pause the game, asked him to do the chore within 30 minutes so he could find a place to stop in the game, and asked him to confirm what I said. If I had done so, we both would have clearly understood what I was asking, and I would not have become frustrated.

Ending the Conversation on a Clear Note

Ask your son or daughter to explain what they think you
  agreed on.
Restate what he or she said if correct.
If that isn't what you agreed to, clarify and explain.
Ask him or her to restate what you said.
If needed, write down any next steps.

Note: I've known parents who write agreements with their kids, with signatures.

Ask Lots of Questions

Questions can facilitate communication far more successfully than statements. Questions reflect an openness to listening. However, there are questions that are more effective than others. Probably one of the least effective questions to start with is "Why did you do that?" In many cases, the answer is "I don't know." Sometimes they do know, but are reluctant to tell you, but oftentimes they don't know. They don't understand why they did it. I remember when my nephew was six. He took his sister's toy, and when I asked him "Why?", he said over and over again that he didn't know. He really didn't, he just did it.

You may ultimately ask that question, but it's better to lead up to it. As you ask questions, use open-ended ones rather than closed questions. If the answer is yes or no, it limits the information you will get from your son or daughter. If you do ask a closed question, quickly follow-up with "Can you tell me more about that?"

A common situation is to ask your kid "What did you learn in school today?" How often have you hear, "Nothing." A better approach is to ask, "What is something you did in school today?"

"We did some writing." "Really, that sounds interesting. What did you write about?" *"Just stuff."* Continue to probe for more details, with a focus on what he or she did, vs. what he or she learned. Suggest that he or she is the expert, and you want to learn. Using this strategy will lead to increased communication, even if it is slower.

Another scenario in which questions are important is when your son or daughter comes to you with a problem. Your first instinct may be to provide a solution, but that typically shuts down the conversation and indicates that you aren't interested in your kid's thoughts. Asking questions to help your son or daughter process the issue and move toward a solution not only is a more effective communication strategy, it also encourages ownership and independence.

Mixed Messages

"What do you think? Oh, you are probably thinking this . . ."
"How do you want to handle this? [Without pausing] I would do . . ."

Take a Risk

If you want to enhance your communication and relationship with your kid, take a risk by sharing personal experiences. I know many parents of teenagers who are reluctant to share their own experiences in high school, whether related to drugs, alcohol, sexual activity, or other controversial experiences. They are afraid their son or daughter will think less of them, or will think because their parents did it, that makes it okay. One of my good friends, Aaliya, led what she terms a "wild lifestyle" in college. As we were discussing this book, she noted that when her daughter was older, she will share with her daughter some examples of things she had done, especially those she regretted. Aaliya believes that by discussing her own experiences, she will be able to more authentically guide her daughter's decision-making. Yes, she is risking a negative reaction from her daughter, but she also risks building a stronger, more genuine relationship.

Encourage Further Communication

Ultimately, you want to encourage further, ongoing conversations with your kids. As I noted earlier, your overall goal should be to reinforce your commitment to open discussion. Incorporating all the strategies we have discussed is important, but another basic tenet is to regularly provide opportunities for communication. You'll want to be available to talk with your son or daughter anytime he or she wants to share, but another key is to build in regular time for communication.

Options for Communication Times

Meal times without phones or TVs
Driving in the car without radio, DVDs, etc.
Weekly family meetings.
Parent "date night" with individual kid.
Social media sessions (family members
    share highlights from their social media).
    **this is in addition to any monitoring.*

Summary

+ Your relationship with your kid should be a top priority.
+ Spend time connecting with your son or daughter.
+ Take time to effectively communicate with your kid, which includes lots of listening.
+ Stay calm, positive, and supportive when your son or daughter is upset.

Classroom Connection

Is there something I might ask my kid's teacher(s) about?

- ◆ From your perspective, how is my relationship with my son or daughter?
- ◆ Is there anything you can share with me that would strengthen my relationship with my son or daughter?
- ◆ Are there any communication tips or strategies that you have found to be particularly effective with my son or daughter?

Are there any ideas I might share with my kid's teacher(s)?

- ◆ Anything about your relationship that might be affecting his or her learning.
- ◆ Your strategies for effectively communicating with your son or daughter.
- ◆ A description of the important relationships in your son's or daughter's life.

4

Myth Four

Expectations for Your Child Are Not Important

As I explained in Chapter 2, success is an important component of our kid's motivation. How we, and they, define success is critical. If we set the bar too high, our kids may feel like they are being set up for failure. If they see a goal as unattainable, they'll give up before they start. On the other hand, if the bar is too low, our kids begin to believe that we don't think they can achieve at high levels.

Expectations are a difficult balance. It's hard when your son is advanced in reading but struggles in science. Isn't learning just learning? Or, your daughter is a terrific dancer, but she stumbles up the stairs. Your expectations should be based on a realistic view of what your son or daughter can do, as well as a vision of who he or she can be. Norman Vincent Peale points out that we should "Shoot for the moon. Even if you miss, you'll land among the stars." This is a great description of how to set expectations for our kids.

Why Do Expectations Matter?

Our expectations drive our kid's motivation and behavior. He or she will respond to our expectations, both in positive and negative ways. For example, if expectations are unrealistic, our kids may give up, shut down, or act out. If our expectations are low, or if we don't have any expectations, our kids may believe we don't have confidence in them, therefore, they quit trying. I read an anonymous poem that describes this from a kid's perspective.

I don't cause teachers trouble.
My grades have been okay.
I listen in my classes,
And I'm in school every day.

My teachers say I'm average
My parents think so too.
I wish I didn't know that,
'Cause there's lots I'd like to do.
I'd like to build a rocket.
I've a book that tells you how;
And start a stamp collection;
Well, no use in trying now.
'Cause since I found I'm average
I'm just smart enough to see
It means there's nothing special
That I should expect of me.

Our expectations and how we communicate them shapes how our kids will motivate and relate to others, including their own kids. If we always push for perfection and set goals that are not likely to be achieved, our son may respond by expecting perfection from everyone around him, or our daughter may learn to be passive and risk-averse, so as not to fail.

Our expectations impact, either positively or negatively, our relationship with our kid. We discussed the importance of relationship to motivation in Chapter 3. Our relationship with our son or daughter is foundational to motivating him or her. If our expectations are out of balance, we can undermine our relationship.

Are There Different Types of Expectations?

As parents, we have an expectation style. Of course, these are not stagnant; you may find yourself moving back and forth between different types, depending on the specific situation. Let's look at four major expectation styles.

Expectation Styles

Pressure Cooker
Royal Family
Helicopters and Lawnmowers
Yoga

Pressure Cooker

First, although we want to have high expectations for our kids, it is possible to have expectations that are too high. Unfortunately, an all too common issue is parents expecting perfectionism from their kids. Kids feel like they are in a pressure cooker, under enormous stress, and just waiting to explode. In this situation, kids are driven by anxiety, afraid they will disappoint their parents. In the extreme, some kids believe their parents will not love them if they do not meet the expected goals or criteria.

I saw this happen with a friend of mine, Mackenzie. She thrived as a student, graduating second in her class in high school. Academic studies were easy for her, and she assumed it would be the same for her children. She filled her house with books, regularly read to them, talked about the importance of school, and encouraged learning whenever possible. Once they started school, she regularly communicated with their teachers to ensure they were successful.

When Jason, her son, began kindergarten, he struggled, especially with reading and writing. The teacher explained to her that, oftentimes, boys, especially those with later birthdates, can have academic challenges. However, she assured Mackenzie this usually improves over time. The teacher provided additional help, and Mackenzie continued working with Jason at home, increasing reading time and using supplemental learning materials and games she found online. The more Jason struggled, the more Mackenzie did to "help." She even kept flash cards in the car and pulled them out at stoplights. As you can imagine, he did not respond well. Jason became sullen and withdrawn, especially when school was the subject.

The negative cycle continued through elementary school. Perfection was the goal, and it wasn't being met. She hired tutors, met with teachers regularly, set specific homework times, and continued to stress the importance of school and good grades, which resulted in him being moderately successful in school, usually earning Bs. Unfortunately, she expected As, so when he earned a B, she told him he needed to try harder.

As Jason became older and entered middle school, he became more resistant to Mackenzie's efforts, and he began to act out at school and at home. Throughout middle school, she reminded him of the importance of college as well as how his current failures would impact which college he could attend. If he earned an A, she praised him and provided rewards, although these were isolated incidents, since he typically earned Bs and Cs. Jason's tutors explained to Mackenzie that he was trying his best, but it was never enough.

As Jason entered high school, the pressure increased. Mackenzie wanted him to attend a "good" college, and, financially, she needed assistance from scholarships. She felt as though time was running out for him to "turn things around." When he failed a class during his freshman year, she berated him for not doing his best, and she began to punish him for his struggles in schools. Jason became more disengaged and rebellious at school, failed additional classes, and arguments became the norm at home.

As you consider Mackenzie's story, think about it from Jason's point of view. Although he received some affirmation for his efforts from teachers and tutors, he felt like he was never good enough for his mother. Since his sister thrived in school, he saw that Mackenzie preferred his sister, so he withdrew even more. By the time he finished high school, he felt like the stereotypical red-headed stepchild.

The challenge with living with a pressure cooker parent is that our kids learn lessons that are not healthy. First, they believe success is based on performance goals set by others, which can be unrealistic. Second, intrinsic motivation is irrelevant; what other people want is more important. Third, kids realize they do not have control in some situations since, once again, the measuring stick is external, and perhaps arbitrary or inappropriate.

The result of living in a pressure cooker? Kids tend to have lower self-esteem, seek approval from others, at times to an unhealthy level, and have mental and physical health problems. Of course, this doesn't happen with every kid, but it does happen with many kids whose parents set unrealistic expectations.

Royal Family

On the other extreme, we sometimes create a royal family for our kids. In this situation, we treat our sons and daughters as kings and queens. In other words, they are royalty; whatever they want is fine, and we cater to their every need. We treat them as if they are the center of the universe, and they respond by expecting everyone to regard them in a similar manner.

How does this work? When Jonathan and Michelle's son was born, they were ecstatic as were grandparents and other extended family members. He was the first grandchild, and the result of many years of attempts to conceive. Everyone showered Bobby with attention, praise, and gifts. As a toddler, he learned that if he cried or screamed, someone would immediately attend to his needs. Several years ago, I watched Bobby and Jonathan throw a ball back and forth in the front yard. Bobby dropped the ball, and it rolled about five feet away from him. He looked at the ball, then started to cry. Jonathan immediately ran to the ball and gave it back to him. This became a regular occurrence, and Jonathan began to learn how to be helpless.

As he grew up, the royal attention continued. In school and sports activities, Jonathan and Michelle regularly met with teachers, principals, and coaches to describe Bobby's unique talents, and how he needed special attention. If Bobby didn't want to follow rules, his parents would ask that the rules be waived for him. Jonathan, Michelle, and all other family members showered him with attention, praising him, even if he didn't do his best.

As a member of a royal family, Bobby began to believe several concepts. First, he was more important than anyone else. Therefore, he should be treated differently from others. Related to that, the rules didn't apply to him. Next, if other people didn't treat him in a special way, they were not people he should care about. Finally, his motivation came from the affirmations and attention of others, not internal drives.

Helicopters and Lawnmowers

You may have heard the term "helicopter parents." It is used to describe parents who constantly monitor their kids and try to help solve problems. In other words, these are parents who "hover" like a helicopter, and when they see an issue, they jump like a paratrooper into the situation.

Alissa, a mother from my church, fits this pattern. She constantly monitors what her daughter, Jasmine, is doing, accompanying her daughter to activities, generally staying nearby, just out of sight. If something doesn't go Jasmine's way, Alissa tries to solve the problem, whether than means talking with a group leader or gymnastics coach, or calling the parents of another teen. Jasmine doesn't want this and is often embarrassed by her mother's behavior. However, she learns a clear lesson: mom will handle all my problems. Therefore, she is not motivated to learn on her own or handle situations independently.

"Lawnmower parents" is a term that has come into the spotlight recently. Similar to helicopter parents, lawnmower parents closely monitor what their kids are doing. In this case, however, instead of jumping in to solve real or perceived problems, they anticipate potential difficulties, and try to mow down, or clear a path for them free of obstacles. The goal is to ensure that their sons and daughters do not experience any struggles; they want to ensure a smooth road to success.

Stephanie Samar, a clinical psychologist at the Mood Disorders Center of the Child Mind Institute, explained the concept in an interview with *Good Morning America*. "If you say, 'Oh, I took care of this for you,' it inadvertently gives that message of 'you can't do this yourself, you can't succeed.'" She also told *Good Morning America* that focusing on short-term parenting goals will take away from the practice of important, long-term goals that kids can benefit from like resiliency, grit, problem-solving, conflict resolution, and coping skills (https://abcnews.go.com/GMA/Family/move-helicopter-moms-lawnmower-parents-rise/story?id=57805055).

I think that most helicopter and lawnmower parents have good intentions. Perhaps they experienced debilitating failure in their lives, or they may have felt isolated or abandoned by their parents. Their goal is to help their kids, and to make life a little easier. However, when we do this, the short-term result is that our kids do not know how to handle challenges, which may result in feelings of helplessness, anxiety, fear, or panic. In the extreme, our kids may deal with mental health issues or addictions as they look for options to escape the challenges of life.

Yoga

Yoga parents fall between the extremes we have discussed. They are balanced in their expectations, finding ways to encourage their kids to dream big dreams, while supporting them to also be realistic.

My best friend, Abbigail, generally fits this profile. She is the first to tell you there are times she puts too much pressure on her kids, and there may be times she hovers a bit too much, but generally, she looks for a balance.

For example, her daughter Asheland just started middle school. Concerned with all the challenges that occur during these years, she started discussing middle school with Asheland starting in 5th grade. Abbigail shared her own experiences, general ideas about middle school, and possible extracurricular activities. At the start of the year, Asheland became excited about becoming a member of the volleyball team. She practiced and began to look forward to the tryouts. Abbigail was encouraging, but also reminded Asheland that many girls would try out, and there would be a limited number that would make the team.

From talking to other parents, Abbigail knew that many of the girls had played on a community team; therefore, they would have an advantage.

Rather than trying to solve this problem for her or insisting that she make the team "or else," Abbigail listened, encouraged, and also asked about other ways Asheland could participate in school activities. One day, Asheland came home and told her mother that her homeroom teacher nominated her to be on the Student Council. Although Asheland was totally focused on volleyball, Abbigail suggested she consider doing both activities. She agreed, and when she did not make the volleyball team, the blow was softened a bit due to her role on the Student Council. Abbigail was also there to focus on the positive, reminding her daughter that she did try, didn't give up, and learned from the experience. Finally, she encouraged Asheland to participate in the community league.

How does this expectation style affect our kids? First, they learn that they can have goals, and, even if they are not successful, that doesn't mean they are failures. Abbigail reinforced the positive aspects of the tryout process, helping Asheland recognize that success is more than making the team. Next, Asheland realized that doing your best in itself is worth celebrating, even if you don't meet an external measurement. Finally, she understood that motivation should come from within, not from outside recognition. Based on this, she plans to hone her skills and try out again next year.

Mixed Messages

I'll take care of it for you [all the time].
Sure [agreeing without listening].

How Can I Set Appropriate Expectations?

This information prompts the question: What can I do as a parent to set appropriate expectations? Let's look at five strategies for doing so.

Five Strategies for Setting Appropriate Expectations

1. Set high expectations without demanding perfection.
2. Encourage your kid without pressure.
3. Support your kid, but don't enable.
4. Help your kid manage his or her expectations of himself or herself.
5. Communicate your philosophy of expectations to others involved in your kid's life.

Set High Expectations Without Demanding Perfection

First, it's important to set high expectations without demanding perfection. As we discussed in the pressure cooker section, expecting perfection puts too much pressure on our kids. Over time, they learn that their efforts are not important; only a flawless outcome is good enough. Then, they come to believe that your love is conditional on good grades, winning, or finishing first and that you do not love them for themselves.

There are many stories of kids who struggled socially or academically who went on to become successful adults. This teaches us to take a longer view of our kids. What we are seeing right now does not fully determine the future. For example, I spoke with a parent who was very concerned that her daughter Selena was not doing well in kindergarten. She moved Selena to a private school with a strong focus on academics, hired a tutor, took Selena to weekly academic learning sessions at a national company, and encouraged all family members to give learning tools for holiday and birthday gifts. By the 3rd grade, Selena was working at grade level, so her mom was content. However, by middle school, Selena was struggling again. What we find is that rushing development by overloading a kid does not last. Ironically, as an adult, Selena owns a small business and is considered successful by any criteria other than school grades.

As another example, my mother continues to be amazed by my current career. In addition to writing, I speak internationally to groups, small and large. She remembers how shy I was while growing up. I was quite introverted, risk-averse, worried I didn't fit in, and afraid to call attention to myself by talking in front of others. That's a stark difference from my current confidence, willingness to travel to new countries, and ability to speak to audiences with over 1,000 participants. Who I was then did not determine who I am now.

So, how do you keep your expectations appropriately high? First, focus on your kid's efforts, not his or her accomplishments. It's fine to praise an accomplishment, whether it is winning a game, making a new friend, or earning a good grade. However, in addition, please recognize and applaud your son's or daughter's efforts to get to know a neighbor's kid, even if they aren't best friends or his or her attempts to clean his or her bedroom, even if it's not the way you want it.

Amy Morin, in 13 Things Mentally Strong Parents Don't Do: Raising Self-assured Children and Training Their Brains for a Life of Happiness, Meaning, and Success, provides a list of warning signs that show you are putting too much pressure on your kids. I've adapted that to a set of guideposts to indicate that you have found a good balance for high expectations.

Five Guideposts for Appropriate High Expectations

1. You praise more than you criticize, focusing on what your kid is doing right.
2. You focus on your child's efforts without comparing them to other kids.
3. You take situations in stride, providing appropriate guidance and support, without overemphasizing failures.
4. You stay calm and collected, especially when your son or daughter isn't performing as you would like.
5. You provide autonomy for your kids rather than trying to control or micromanage their lives.

Mixed Messages

I'm proud of you for making an A; too bad you didn't make
an A+.

That's a good start, but it's not quite what your older sister
did.

Encourage Your Kid Without Pressure

Next, we need to balance our expectations with encouragement to help our kids be successful. The main strategy that encourages our kids is to authentically emphasize the positive. Encouragement differs a bit from praise as we noted in Chapter 1. Praise recognizes success; encouragement also recognizes effort whether your kids are successful or not. For example, you may encourage your high school son by saying, "I realize you are disappointed with your grade on your group project. But I also noticed your teacher also commented on how well you work with others, and that you took a leadership role in the group. That is terrific and will help you later in life."

A related concept is to help your kids learn and improve without pressure. Kavin was struggling on her soccer team. Her dad praised her efforts, but continually told her what to do to improve. Kavin interpreted this as her dad saying she didn't know what to do and he was going to "fix her." As you might imagine, this was not a positive situation.

Encouragement also means that you will urge your kids to push through a struggle when they are simply overwhelmed, but if they have become totally disengaged, you help them find an alternative. If your daughter tries and tries to play the piano and ultimately is so frustrated that she has developed a negative attitude about learning anything new, it's probably time to take a break or stop.

Watch Out for Competition

Another key strategy is to deemphasize competition, which I'll address in Chapter 7. For now, keep in mind that the more you compare your son or daughter to siblings, neighbors, classmates, peers, or teammates, the more you reinforce that he or she will not be good enough.

Support Your Kid, But Don't Enable

It is appropriate to support your kids. If they are participating in a sport, practicing with them at home can be beneficial. If they are struggling at school, talking with their teacher, arranging for tutoring with the teacher, and helping with homework are homework. However, if we aren't careful, we begin to solve their problems for them. I can't count the number of parents who completed a project for one of my students. They could have provided suggestions or guidance, assisted with finding resources, or asked questions, but they did the majority of the project. That is enabling your kid.

Additionally, when your kid is struggling, whether it is with a relationship, chores, school, or other activities, be careful that you are not enabling your son or daughter by allowing him or her to become overwhelmed by emotions. Mark, a colleague of mine, faced this situation with his daughter as she entered middle school. Every day she came home from school with a crisis. Sometimes it was related to academics, sometimes a classmate wouldn't sit with her at lunch, and, at times, she experienced another type of negative situation. Although Mark quickly addressed major issues such as bullying, he recognized a pattern of catastrophizing incidents. As they talked, Alissa explained in depth how she felt and how bad it was and how the world would end. She also described how everything was someone else's fault, and she couldn't do anything about it. Although it is important to talk about feelings, they were like a tidal wave, overtaking everything, and she began to develop a victim mentality. Once he realized that by only listening to her reaction, he was enabling a negative perspective, Mark began to guide the conversation with a focus on what happened and how Alissa could address it if it happened again. This shift helped

Alissa focus on herself as a strong problem-solver, without an over-dependence on her father.

Guiding Questions

What happened? Describe the actual situation?
What did you do? How did you respond?
Was that the best thing you should have done? How do you know?
If this happens again, what will you do differently?

A final part of appropriate support is to help your kids handle situations independently. If you ask your son to vacuum the living room, after you know he understands what to do, leave him alone to complete the task. If you hover and try to micromanage him, he'll never learn to try things for himself. Or, if your daughter is struggling at school or in an extracurricular activity, talk to the teacher or adviser/coach for input, but don't solve the challenge for your daughter.

Mixed Messages

I want you to do this on your own but let me help just a little.
I'm sorry that happened to you. It happened to me one time too. Here's what I did.

Help Your Kid Manage His or Her Expectations of Himself or Herself

There are times that you have reasonable expectations of your kid, but he or she has an unrealistic view of himself or herself. This happens most often when kids think they must be perfect. I remember teaching Jasmine, who wanted to have the best grade in the class. She told me her parents expected that of her, and that she would be in trouble if she ever scored less than an A. During parent conferences, I brought this up to them, and they were stunned. They had never put pressure on her about grades. However, she felt the need to be perfect, and didn't want to admit it was an internal burden.

You also may have a kid who has low expectations of himself or herself. Pat, one of the professors at my university, faced this situation with her daughter. She wasn't doing well in math, and when Pat asked her about it, Brenda responded, "Don't you know? Girls aren't as good as boys in math." She used a common misconception to excuse her lack of attention to the subject. In this case, you'll want to share examples of females who thrive in math careers, explain why that isn't true, and find engaging ways to help her see that she can learn.

In another situation, Reid's son Mikey was on the basketball team. He was lackadaisical, putting forth minimal effort. His coach knew that Mikey's older brother Kevin had been the team captain a few years back, but he assumed that Kevin was helping Mikey with his attitude and skills. Kevin did help, but Reid felt he could never live up to Kevin, so he didn't try. As with any competition, even if it is self-imposed, there can be negative outcomes. Be careful to help your son or daughter focus (and refocus) on his or her own efforts.

Communicate Your Philosophy of Expectations to Others Involved in Your Kid's Life

Finally, share how you feel about expectations with teachers, coaches, extended families, and any other adults in your kid's life. A friend of mine co-parents her son with her ex-husband. Julia is focused on her son succeeding academically, but she is careful not to pressure Eli. However, her ex-husband continually tells Eli that school is not important, he doesn't need to do his homework, and that he should focus on playing football, since that would help him gain admission to college. Eli was interested in school and football but felt as though he was picking a particular parent if he only focused on one. Julia and her ex-husband sat down together and agreed on a plan to encourage Eli in both areas. Although a common issue in divorced families, I've seen similar situations with a relative, such as an uncle or grandparent, a sponsor of an extracurricular activity, such as a band director, or other adults who just want to help. They may not listen, but ask for their help in supporting your philosophy.

Summary

- ◆ Balance your expectations for your kid; you want them to be high, but not at a completely unattainable level, such as perfection.
- ◆ Assess the messages you send your son or daughter through your parenting style and adjust it if needed.
- ◆ Encourage achievement of goals without pressure.
- ◆ Help your kid develop his or her own balanced expectations of himself or herself.

Classroom Connection

Is there something I might ask my kid's teacher(s) about?

- ◆ What are your expectations for my son or daughter?
- ◆ How do you communicate expectations to your students?
- ◆ How can I help my kid balance your expectations with those of their peers, family members, or other adults?

Are there any ideas I might share with my kid's teacher(s)?

- ◆ Your expectations for your kid related to school and learning.
- ◆ How you communicate to adults and other family members about your expectations.

5

Myth Five

It's Okay for Your Kid to Fail All the Time

Failure is a natural part of life. However, it can affect your kid's motivation. If kids learn from a failure or mistake, it increases motivation and encourages growth and appropriate risk-taking. If it is overwhelmingly negative, it can paralyze your son or daughter. If you want to motivate your kid, you need to help him or her see failures in a positive way so that he or she learns how to handle setbacks, persist through challenges, and ultimately achieve goals.

How kids view mistakes reflects how they feel about failure. Some people view failure as a stop sign, signaling you should give up. However, we all know people who have made a mistake or failed in some way, learned a lesson, and later became successful. You might share information about these people at dinner, in the car, or on public transportation.

Three People Who Have Overcome Failure

Viola Davis

Making television history, Viola Davis became the first African American woman to win an Emmy Award for best actress. She took home this important honor in 2015 for her portrayal of Annalise Keating in the legal drama *How to Get Away With Murder*. Davis had overcome great obstacles to reach the stage and accept that prestigious honor. She grew up in poverty in Rhode Island. Davis "didn't know where the next meal was coming from," according to *US Magazine*. "I did everything to get food," she explained.

Davis also had to contend with a lot of racial prejudice as a child. She and her family were the only African Americans in their community, and she found herself being teased by her classmates because of her race. Davis found inspiration in African American actresses such as Cicely Tyson.

Excerpt from: www.biography.com/news/african-american-women-who-changed-history

Steve Jobs

You always hear about a "long road to the top," but perseverance isn't limited to the early stages of a person's career. Oftentimes, failure can occur after a long period of success.

Steve Jobs achieved great success at a young age. When he was 20 years old, Jobs started Apple in his parents' garage, and within a decade the company blossomed into a $2 billion empire. However, at age 30, Apple's board of directors decided to take the business in a different direction, and Jobs was fired from the company he created. Jobs found himself unemployed, but treated it as a freedom rather than a curse. In fact, he later said that getting fired from Apple was the best thing to ever happen to him, because it allowed him to think more creatively and reexperience the joys of starting a company.

Jobs went on to found NeXT, a software company, and Pixar, the company that produces animated movies such as *Finding Nemo*. NeXT was subsequently purchased by Apple. Not only did Jobs go back to his former company, but he helped launch Apple's current resurgence in popularity. Jobs claims that his career success and his strong relationship with his family are both results of his termination from Apple.

Excerpt from: www.growthink.com/content/7-entrepreneurs-whose-perseverance-will-inspire-you

J.K. Rowling

J.K. Rowling, author of the *Harry Potter* books, is currently the second-richest female entertainer on the planet, behind Oprah Winfrey. However, when Rowling wrote the first *Harry Potter* book in 1995, 12 different publishers rejected it. Even Bloomsbury, the small publishing house that finally purchased Rowling's manuscript, told the author to "get a day job."

At the time when Rowling was writing the original *Harry Potter* book, her life was a self-described mess. She was going through a divorce and living in a tiny flat with her daughter. Rowling was surviving on government subsidies, and her mother had just passed away from multiple sclerosis. Rowling turned these negatives into a positive by devoting most of her free time to the *Harry Potter* series. She also drew from her bad personal experiences when writing. The result is a brand name currently worth nearly $15 billion.

Excerpt from: www.growthink.com/content/7-entrepreneurs-whose-perseverance-will-inspire-you

I'm a passionate college basketball fan, especially of Duke University. One thing I've noticed is that whenever they lose a game or don't play their best, they practice harder. They use failure to motivate themselves to improve, and that's what we want for our kids.

Mixed Messages

That's great that you learned about someone who was successful; that's really not something that happens very often.

How Do Kids Cope With Failure?

Kids not only view failure differently, they also react in various ways. According to UC Berkeley professor Martin Covington (Simmons, 2018), kids generally fall into four categories as to how they cope with failure. See if you recognize any of your kids in the descriptions.

Success-Oriented Students	*Overstrivers*
These are the kids who love learning for the sake of learning and see failure as a way to improve their ability rather than a slight on their value as a human being. Research has also found that these students tend to have parents who praise success and rarely, if ever, reprimand failure.	These students are what Covington calls the "closet-achievers." They avoid failure by succeeding—but only with herculean effort motivated solely by the fear that even one failure will confirm their greatest fear: that they're not perfect. Because the fear of failure is so overpowering and because they doubt their abilities, Overstrivers will, on occasion, tell everyone that they have very little time to prepare for an upcoming test—and then spend the entire night studying. When they pass the test with flying colors, this "shows" everyone that they are brilliant because their "ability" trumped the need to extend any effort.

Failure-avoiding	Failure-accepting
These students don't expect to succeed—they just want to avoid failing. They believe that if they extend a lot of effort but still fail, then this implies low ability and hence, low worth. But if they don't try and still fail, this will not reflect negatively on their ability and their worth remains intact.	These are the hardest students to motivate because they've internalized failure—they believe their repeated failures are due to lack of ability and have given up on trying to succeed and thus maintain their self-worth. Any success they might experience they ascribe to circumstances outside their control such as the teacher giving them the easiest task in a group project.
In order to avoid failure that might be due to lack of ability, they do things such as make excuses (the dog ate my homework), procrastinate, don't participate, and choose near-impossible tasks. However, this can put them into a tricky position when they encounter a teacher who rewards effort and punishes for what appears to be lack of effort or worse. Ultimately, there's no way out for these students—either they try and fail or they're punished.	

What Is Growth Mindset and Why Does It Matter?

Growth mindset is another area that is important to consider. What a kid believes about his or her potential for learning matters. If Ricardo believes that he can be successful with new concepts, especially if he puts forth effort, that growth mindset will help him be more likely to succeed. On the other hand, if Kelly thinks that you are either smart or you aren't, which is a fixed mindset, she is unlikely to try to learn new things, and she is less likely to succeed. Let's look at mindset in the graphic that follows.

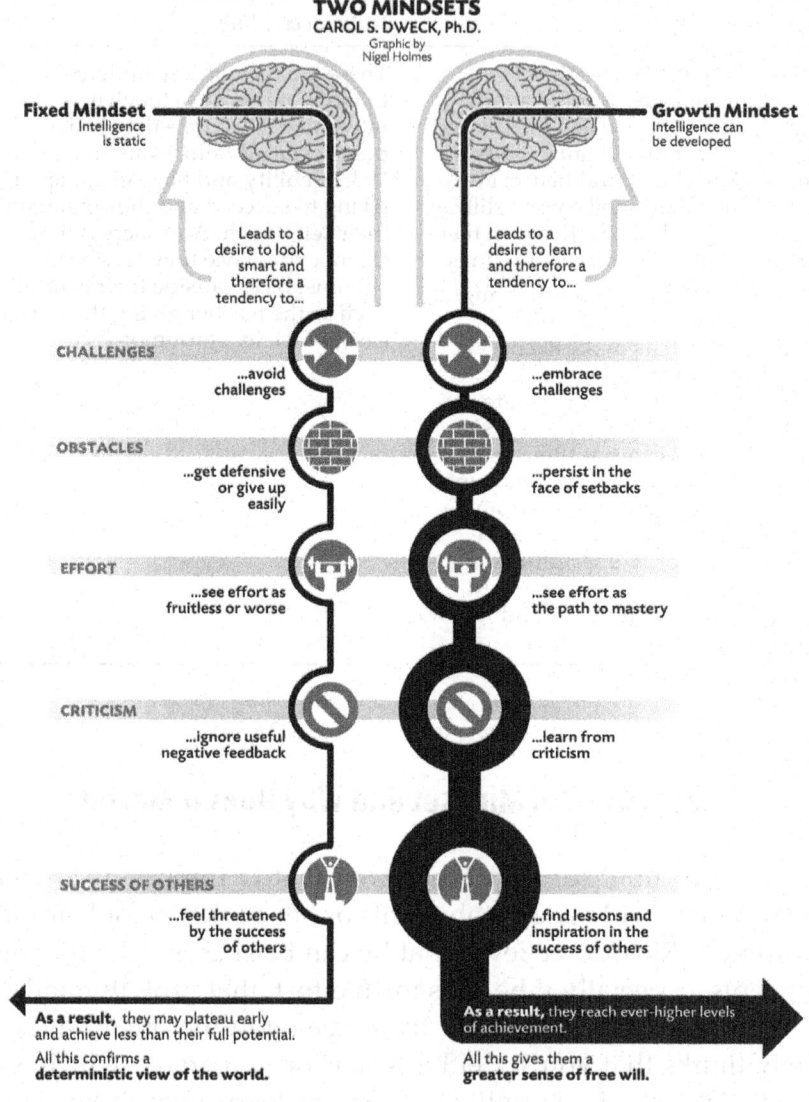

Growth Mindset vs. Fixed Mindset

Understanding the growth mindset aspects for kids can help you motivate and support them. Using a series of statements, you can assess whether your son or daughter has a strong or weak growth mindset, or a fixed mindset. For younger kids, you will want to use the assessment orally, for elementary age kids, use the yes/no version, and for middle and high schoolers, you can use the scaled version for your assessment as well as student self-assessment. Keep in mind you don't need to use the written assessment, you can just discuss the information at dinner or in the car.

Elementary Growth Mindset Assessment

	Yes	No
If you are smart, you don't have to try hard.	☺	☹
The harder you work, the smarter you will be.	☺	☹
I can learn new things, but it doesn't mean I'm smart; I'm just lucky.	☺	☹
Only some people are really good at certain subjects, like math.	☺	☹
If something is too hard, I give up because I'm not smart enough.	☺	☹
I like it when work is easy for me.	☺	☹
I like learning when I have to think hard.	☺	☹
If someone gives me feedback about something I can improve, I get upset.	☺	☹
If I don't know what to do, that means I'm not smart enough.	☺	☹
I don't like trying new things, especially if they look hard.	☺	☹
I'll ask for help if I need it.	☺	☹

Middle/High School Growth Assessment

	Strongly Disagree	Disagree	I Don't Know	Agree	Strongly Agree
If you are smart, you don't have to try hard.					
The harder you work, the smarter you will be.					

(Continued)

(Continued)

	Strongly Disagree	Disagree	I Don't Know	Agree	Strongly Agree
I can learn new things, but it doesn't mean I'm smart; I'm just lucky.					
Only some people are really good at certain subjects, like math.					
If something is too hard, I give up because I'm not smart enough.					
I like it when work is easy for me.					
I like learning when I have to think hard.					
If someone gives me feedback about something I can improve, I get upset.					
If I don't know what to do, that means I'm not smart enough.					
I don't like trying new things, especially if they look hard.					
I'll ask for help if I need it.					

You may want to give this assessment to your kid's teacher(s) so they can gauge your kid's growth and changes.

Mixed Messages

You're really good at swimming; you were born with a special talent.

You are so smart you don't even need to study.

Reinforce Effort

Encouraging and reinforcing effort are particularly important to build a growth mindset in your kids. Kids often do not understand the role effort plays in success. In *Classroom Instruction that Works*, Marzano, Pickering, and Pollock (2001) make two important comments regarding students' views about effort which can help parents assist their kids in overcoming failure.

Research-Based Generalizations About Effort

♦ Not all students realize the importance of believing in effort.

♦ Students can learn to change their beliefs to an emphasis on effort.

(Marzano et al., 2001, p. 50)

This is positive news for parents and teachers. First, we're not imagining it—kids don't realize they need to exert effort. And second, we can help them change that belief. I think our words make a big difference in encouraging or discouraging effort. Claudia Mueller and Carol Dweck, researchers at Columbia University, found that, when adults praise intelligence or ability in a kid, that kid will put forth less effort, because he or she assumes he or she already has the capability to do the work, so why try harder? This leads to a decrease in achievement. On the other hand, when we reinforce effort, "Wow, I can tell you worked hard on your science homework and it looks like it is making a difference," students will try harder, which leads to an increase in achievement.

How Can I Help My Kids Develop Grit and Perseverance?

What Is Grit and Why Is It Important?

Grit is an important part of dealing with failure. Grit is the notion of endurance—being persistent and putting forth effort to move forward, despite obstacles. Angela L. Duckworth and James J. Gross (2014) propose a mathematical way to think how grit leads to achievement, whether in school, other activities, or life.

Grit = Effort
Talent × Effort = Skill
Skill × Effort = Achievement

You may be wondering why I'm addressing grit while we are discussing failure. As kids face obstacles and failures in school, when pursuing interests such as sports, band, drama, or music, or in social situations, such as making new friends, grit is a necessary skill. Learning how to persist in new or challenging situations also helps your kid develop resilience and prepares kids for life. There are four benefits of developing grit for your kid.

Grit

Goal Achievement
Real-Life Preparation
Identification of Struggles and Strategies for Persistence
Talent Appreciation, While Also Recognizing the Importance of Effort

How Can I Tell If My Kid Has Grit?

Once we understand the what and why of grit, we need to address what grit actually looks like in our kids. How can I know if my kids are gritty? Let's look at some specific behaviors you can observe.

Descriptors of Kids with Grit	Descriptors of Kids without Grit
Are willing to tackle new tasks, projects, and situations	Give up before they start on something
When challenges arise, they are willing to persist	Give up immediately when there is a challenge
Are willing to take reasonable, safe risks to accomplish a goal	Don't take reasonable risks or take unsafe risks
Recognize and learn from their part in success or failure	Blame others for struggle
Realizing the difference between sharing feelings and being overly negative	Use negative talk with themselves or others
Are willing to explore open-ended tasks and situations, and enjoy the ability to explore	Do not like any task that is not specifically spelled out step-by-step
Appreciate the positive affirmation for progress and effort, but do not expect praise or credit unless earned	Want credit, even when task is not completed or effort was not exerted

Mixed Messages

That looks like it is really hard. Why don't you do something else instead?

You worked really hard [when he or she didn't].

How Can I Help My Kid Develop Grit?

Lee David Daniels, in his book *Grit for Kids: 16 Top Steps for Developing Grit, Passion, Willpower, and Perseverance in Kids for Self-confidence and a Successful Life* shares two ways of developing grit, as originally described by Angela Duckworth. In some ways, these are similar to intrinsic and extrinsic motivation. First, you can grow grit from the inside, which occurs when you create a vision and tie activities to that vision, build on your interests, and practice your skills. Second, you can develop grit from the outside, which involves all those people around your kid, how they support kids attempting challenges, encouraging interests, and demonstrating grit in their lives.

From an outside, or external, perspective, there are six strategies you can use to help your son or daughter develop or strengthen grit.

Allow boredom.
Model and share your own experiences.
Allow mistakes to encourage problem-solving.
Provide a supportive environment.
Give options for choice.
Don't take away hope.

First, it's important to allow your kid to be bored. That is very difficult in our tech-heavy society, and it may sound counterintuitive. After all, we don't want to give them opportunities to "get into trouble." We often overschedule our kids, running them from one activity to another. However, if their hands, bodies, and minds are always working at 100%, there isn't any time to reflect. A part of grit is building an interest in a skill or topic, and unless our kids have some time to think about their interests, and develop them at a deep level, they aren't able to develop a passion, which is critical to grit.

Kids also need to see models of grit. We all have struggles, as well as strategies for persevering in the face of struggles. Based on your kid's age, have an appropriate discussion about what is happening in your life, whether it is seeking a job or a new job, or balancing the budget. Also discuss past situations you have faced. In the discussions, share how you were able to persist and overcome challenges. It's also helpful for other adults, such as relatives, coaches, or teachers to share their experiences.

When your son or daughter is working through a new task or situation, allow mistakes. This encourages problem-solving. Do you remember when we discussed lawnmower parents? They are so intent on protecting their kids they try to prevent mistakes. That does a disservice to our kids, and teaches them to avoid failure, which isn't practical. Allow the mistakes, then coach them to move past it. Rather than saying "I would solve that problem this way," ask "How would you solve it? What did you do in class that can help you? Have you ever seen a similar problem?" When we provide answers to our kids, we are taking away their opportunity to learn how to solve problems and their chance to practice grit.

Next, create a supportive environment. For example, if your child demonstrates interest in a topic or activity, provide opportunities for him or her to pursue his or her interest. This may involve providing transportation to an activity, providing needed supplies, or paying a fee for an outside activity, such as a camp. As I said in Chapter 3, you'll have to work within your financial means, so look for cost-effective alternatives.

Another important strategy is to give your son or daughter choices. This may be allowing them to choose between extra activities, the place to complete their homework, or the level of challenge of an activity. There are two important notes here. First, allowing them to choose outside activities, such as a club or sport, can be a two-edged sword. You are allowing them to pick what they want to do, but that interest may wane, and they quit. The daughter of a friend, Luz, wanted to compete in cheerleading. Amparo mainly joined because a friend was competing, so she quit when she wasn't winning. Next, she wanted to learn to dance like another friend, so Luz registered her for dance lessons. Within a few weeks, Amparo wanted to quit, because she didn't feel successful (Chapter 2). Luz's husband was frustrated and shared his concern that if they continued to let her quit, she would never learn to be persistent. They had a conversation with Amparo and explained why she needed to continue with dance. If she was not happy after two months, they would allow her to quit. Any future activities would require a minimum of a two-month commitment.

Another aspect of choice is to consider the level of challenge of a task or activity. We don't want to discourage our kids from dreaming big, but we also want our sons and daughters to have at least some chance of success. Look for a balance: tasks or activities should be difficult enough that kids are learning something new, but not so hard that they give up. If you like to play tennis, you'll improve if you play against someone who is better than you. But if you play against Venus and Serena Williams, you'll learn less because you are overwhelmed by their advanced skill level.

I'd like to share an example of developing grit in the classroom. It's important to allow students to actually practice using grit. This one is a bit tricky. Teachers must know their students well enough to know how much frustration they can handle, and then provide them a learning opportunity in which they will struggle. Quick success is not the goal in crafting the activity; providing students an opportunity to feel frustrated and respond is.

Thomas Hoerr (2013) describes an effective process to use when presenting students with a learning opportunity to develop grit.

1. Create frustration
   a. Before they start, ask students to anticipate how hard the assignment might be and to think about something else they have done at the same level.
   b. Next, ask them to think about a task when they were successful and how grit played a role.
   c. Then, have students work on the assignment with five minutes of full force effort. When they struggle, they should stop and breathe, reflect, and try something else.
   d. Remind students that a good failure is one where you learn. What are you learning?
2. Monitor the experience
   a. Gauge how frustrated they are using a simple scale (numbers or just up and down).
   b. Ask how they respond to frustration. Place them in groups based on the strategies they used for a response. Ask the groups to discuss.
   c. Create checklist to monitor progress. You may want something like a two-column chart with headings of key points in the lesson on the left and a place for

notes on the right. For younger students, you can keep this as the teacher (based on your observations); for older students, they can self-assess.

3. Reflect and learn. Discuss the lessons learned. Then celebrate progress!

Take care with the amount of "grit opportunities" you provide. For many of your struggling learners, everything is a "grit opportunity." These, however, will be structured experiences in which you coach them as to how to respond appropriately. You'll also want to make sure they understand what you are doing and why so they don't give up.

Worth the Risk

I gave an incorrect answer
And you thanked me for taking a chance
You said that by my courage
My knowledge would surely advance
I could have felt embarrassed
But you handled it so well
You reached your hand out just in time
And caught me before I fell
So not only am I still standing
But I'm standing tall and proud
And next time, even if I'm not sure
I'll be willing to risk it aloud.

Annette Breaux
© Annette Breaux. Used with permission.

Finally, don't take away hope. From your perspective, don't discourage your son or daughter from his or her dreams and goals, even if you know it's not viable. For example, Dedric, one of my students, wanted to be a National Football League player. The problem was that, although he was on the football team, he wasn't a very good player. His grades and his football skills were both weak, so playing at the college level was not likely to happen. Based on that, he was extremely unlikely to play for the NFL. Even with a more advanced skill set, most high school students do not become members on an NFL team.

- ◆ High school senior players who go on to play NCAA men's football: about 1 in 17, or 5.8%.
- ◆ NCAA senior players drafted by an NFL team: about 1 in 50, or 2.0%.
- ◆ High school senior players eventually drafted by an NFL team: about 9 in 10,000, or 0.09%.

That's about the chance you have an IQ above 150, as measured by the Stanford-Binet test. The average IQ of Ph.D. students is 130.

Source: Norwich City Schools, Norwich, NY

You might be wondering how I responded to Dedric. I chose not to share statistics with him or try to talk him out of his dream. I encouraged him to talk with his coaches and improve his skills. Then, I encouraged him to focus on academics. When he responded, "I'm going to play football; I don't need to learn this stuff," I explained that learning skills such as reading, writing, math, and problem-solving would help him handle all the other aspects of being a player, such as money management and public relations. I also pointed out that players in the NFL only play for an average of three years, and education would help him prepare for life after football. He didn't necessarily give up on his goal, but he did learn to focus on academics as well.

Next, help your kid avoid the mental traps that can discourage him or her. Model how to escape the trap, and coach him or her through the process.

Mental Trap	How to Escape the Trap
Rigidity: everything should or must be done in a certain way.	Recognize there are a variety of ways to accomplish a task or activity.
Catastrophizing: everything is AWFUL and it will never get better.	Challenges are normal. It may seem bad right now, but I can get through this, perhaps with some help.
Personalizing: because I'm struggling with this, I'm a bad person.	Just because this is hard doesn't mean I'm a bad person. It means that I may not understand what to do or have the appropriate skills.
Helplessness: this is so hard I should just give up. I probably should never have started.	This is hard. I wonder how I can get help (should I ask teacher or parents, look something up on the Internet)?

Summary

- ◆ Teach your kid that failure is a learning experience, not a stop sign.
- ◆ Model and encourage a growth mindset, rather than a fixed one.
- ◆ Reinforce effort whenever possible.
- ◆ Grit is a critical skill that your kid can learn.

Classroom Connection

Is there something I might ask my kid's teacher(s) about?

- ◆ How does my son or daughter cope with mistakes or failure in your class?
- ◆ How do you approach situations when your students make mistakes or fail?
- ◆ How can I help my kid develop a growth mindset?

Are there any ideas I might share with my kid's teacher(s)?

- ◆ How your kid copes with mistakes or failures at home.
- ◆ How you model and encourage grit.
- ◆ Strategies you use to help your kid develop a growth mindset.

6

Myth Six

It's Okay for Your Kid to Get Stuck

In Chapter 5, we discussed the concept of failure. This chapter is closely related, in that we are looking at how to keep moving when failing or feeling like a failure. I recently heard a song called "Field of Failure." That's a great analogy for this notion of failure and getting unstuck. When I was in middle school, I walked to school through a field. There were times I stepped into holes or stumbled in the dirt. It turns out, this is a field of failures, or mistakes. I had to walk through it to get to school, but I didn't have to stay there. That's what we want for our kids; not to avoid the field of failure, but also not to get stuck in it. The ability to "get unstuck" or move on through failure is also called resilience. Resilience is the ability or skill to bounce back when discouraged and move on after learning from a mistake or failure. Some people consider it an ability; I believe it is a skill that can be learned. Throughout this chapter, I'll use resilience and getting unstuck as synonyms. Let's start with the characteristics your kids need in order to be resilient, then we'll move to ways you can help your kids get unstuck.

What Are the Characteristics My Kids Should Have so They Aren't Stuck in a Field of Failure?

In *Building Resilience in Children and Teens*, Kenneth Ginsberg and Martha Jablow (2011) point out there are seven "crucial C's" of resilience: competence, confidence, connection, character, contribution, coping, and control. Think of these as a braided cord, with each strand interwoven with the others. The more of them you have, the stronger you are.

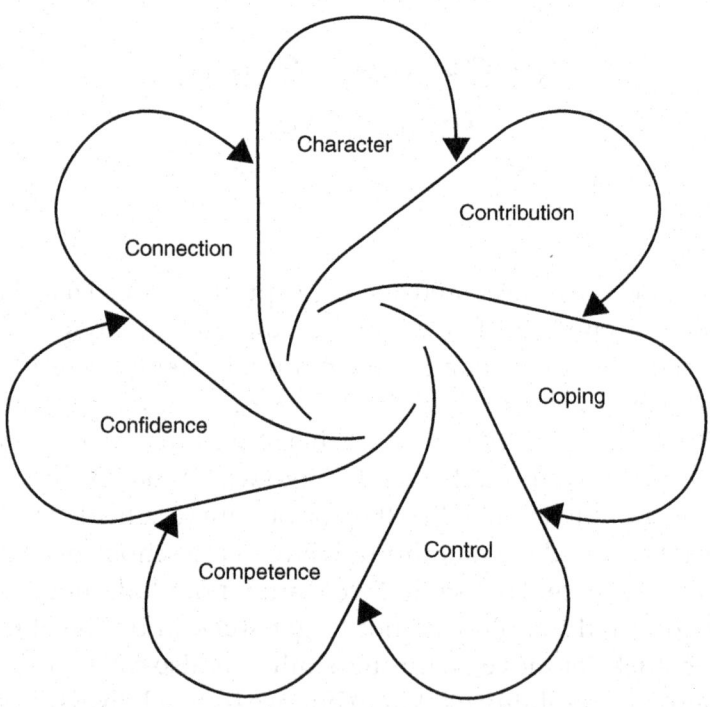

Seven C's

For example, when you feel competent, or successful, that typically builds confidence and intrinsic motivation. Confident kids have a sense of control, which, in turn, helps them cope when they are stuck. Throughout the process, they make connections within themselves and to others and build their character. Ultimately, they share their strategies with others, making a contribution to society. Each is important, but together, they make you stronger. Helping your son or daughter move beyond being stuck in a field of failure requires raising him or her to be resilient.

What Are Some General Strategies for Raising Resilient Kids?

I had a student who was a constant challenge, and I taught him for 2½ years! Todd came into my class with a reputation as an at-risk learner, and in 7th grade he lived up to it. By the 8th grade, he was stuck where he was, despite struggling to move beyond his past patterns and others' preconceived notions of him. The turning point in our student-teacher relationship came when I discovered he had a talent for drawing, and I arranged for him to do some artwork for a special project. I was amazed at the turnaround from a completely negative attitude in my class the prior year to a positive attitude. He used his art to help him process learning. In fact, if other students were struggling, he would share his drawings with them to help them understand.

I'm always reminded of Todd's story when I read my favorite children's book, *The Phantom Tollbooth* by Norton Juster. During their journey, Milo, Tock, and the Humbug end up jumping to the Island of Conclusions, which turns out to be a less-than-pleasant place. I jumped to conclusions about Todd based on our first day of class together, and it took me two years to move past that and build a strong relationship. I regret the wasted time, because I could have made so much more progress with him if I had started our teacher-student learning relationship differently. Making the choice to *not* jump to conclusions is less about our kids than it is about who we are as parents.

"Now will you tell me where we are?" asked Tock as he looked around the desolate island. "To be sure," said Canby; "you're on the Island of Conclusions. Make yourself at home. You're apt to be here for some time." "But how did we get here?" asked Milo, who was still a bit puzzled by being there at all. "You jumped, of course," explained Canby. "That's the way most everyone gets here. It's really quite simple; every time you decide something without having a good reason, you jump to Conclusions whether you like it or not. It's such an easy trip to make that I've been here hundreds of times." "But this is such an unpleasant-looking place," Milo remarked. "Yes, that's true," admitted Canby; "it does look much better from a distance."

From *The Phantom Tollbooth* by Norton Juster

I thought about this story when I was trying to determine what information would be most important for parents to help their kids become resilient. Jumping to conclusions about why your son or daughter is stuck or how he or she should solve his or her problem is typically not helpful.

Mixed Messages

[When son or daughter comes home from school and looks upset; without asking questions] I know exactly what is wrong. Here's what we'll do.

If that is what you shouldn't do, what should you do to help your kids? Robert Brooks and Sam Goldstein (2001) in *Raising Resilient Children* provide ten strategic guideposts for parents (and teachers) who foster resilience.

Ten Guiding Strategies for Raising Resilient Students

1. Being empathetic.
2. Communicating effectively and listening actively.
3. Changing "negative scripts."
4. Loving our children in ways that help them to feel special and appreciated.
5. Accepting our children for who they are and helping them to set realistic expectations and goals.
6. Helping our children experience success by identifying and reinforcing their "islands of competence."
7. Helping children recognize that mistakes are experiences from which to learn.
8. Developing responsibility, compassion, and a social conscience by providing children with opportunities to contribute.
9. Teaching our children to solve problems and make decisions.
10. Disciplining in a way that promotes self-discipline and self-worth.

What Are Specific Strategies I Can Use to Help My Kid Get Unstuck and Become Resilient?

Now that we have discussed some general guideposts, let's look at nine specific strategies you can utilize with your kids.

How to Help Kids Get Unstuck and Become RESILIENT

Remind your son or daughter of the past struggles and successes you and other family members face, struggles of others, and their own struggles.

Encourage problem-solving, not problem-obsession.

Set and track goals and achievements.

Identify specific struggles and address them.

Look out for shortcuts.
Intentionally provide scaffolding.
Encourage preparation to prevent problems.
Nudge in a positive manner.
Teach them how to be self-controlled.

Remind Your Son or Daughter of the Past Struggles and Successes You and Other Family Members Face, Struggles of Others, and Their Own Struggles

The first strategy for helping your son or daughter to get unstuck is to remind him or her of the struggles of others and how they overcame those struggles. This helps your kid recognize that he or she is not the only one who has ever been in this situation, which is a common reaction. Start by sharing your own struggles and strategies for moving past them. I remember one year when I was teaching graduate students at a university. They were all teachers coming to school at night to work on a master's degree. Research writing was a challenge for them. One night, I brought in an article I had written for a journal; one that had been rejected.

I showed them the comments, and then explained what I was going to do to revise and resubmit the article. It was an eye-opener for them. As one of them said, "I never realized you didn't write perfectly all the time!" Our kids don't see us struggle. They think we just magically do what we do. It's important to show them otherwise.

We can also provide role models with stories of people who have persevered. This can be with posters of those people along with a quote exemplifying how they overcame success, or by reading about them. Kids often like to put posters on their walls of people they admire. I like to encourage them to post at least one of someone who has overcome struggles to become successful. You can also use books to teach your kids about resilience.

Young Adult Novels That Teach Grit and Resilience

Sonia Nazario	*Enrique's Journey*
Pam Mynoz Ryan	*Experanza Rising*
Gary Paulsen	*Hatchet*
Sharon Draper	*Out of My Mind*
Chris Crutcher	*Ironman*
Mildred D. Taylor	*Roll of Thunder, Hear My Cry*
Suzanne Collins	*The Hunger Games*
Timothee de Formbelle	*Toby and the Secrets of the Tree*
Lawrence Yep	*Dragonwings*

Children's Literature That Teaches Grit and Resilience

Watty Piper	*The Little Engine That Could*
Mary Hoffman	*Amazing Grace*
Patricia Polacco	*Thank You, Mr. Falker*
Tommie de Paola	*The Art Lesson*
Patty Lovell	*Stand Tall, Molly Lou Melon*
Dr. Seuss	*Horton Hatches an Egg*
Matt Whitlock	*Gigantic Little Hero*
Spike Lee, Tonya Lewis Lee, and Sean Qualls	*Giant Steps to Change the World*
Pat Thomas and Lesley Harker	*I Can Do It! A First Look at Not Giving Up*

Finally, it's important for kids to remember how they dealt with past struggles. I like to keep a success journal, success pages, or a success poster. It's a simple three-column log, which can be decorated if your kid would like.

Three-Column Log

Problem or Struggle	*What I Did*	*How I Succeeded*

Encourage Problem-Solving, Not Problem-Obsession

Next, encourage problem-solving and discourage an obsession with the problem. Kerri, the daughter of a friend of mine, was struggling to make friends. Rather than trying to determine ways to make new friends, she complained everyday about not having friends. Kerri was slated for failure, because she never moved past the problem. Ultimately, Martha, her mother, had multiple conversations to guide her to a solution. Martha asked lots of questions so that Kerri came up with ideas, rather than simply telling her what to do. She was teaching Kerri how to solve the problem on her own.

Set and Track Goals and Achievements

Oftentimes, when we get stuck, it's because the problem is simply too overwhelming. In those cases, we need to break the problem down into smaller goals. I used the graphic on the next page which I adapted from Janet Allen's writing activity, with one of my upper elementary students, Stephen, who responded better to pictures and boxes rather than a blank page. I also used simpler language to be kid-friendly. First, he decided what he wanted to do (upper left, mouth), and why he thought this was best (upper right, brain). On the middle left (hand), he wrote the specific steps or actions to take. Then, Stephen moved to the bottom left (foot) to list what could go right, or what might be the benefits or successes if he took the identified actions. Moving to the bottom right (the Achilles Heel), he listed what could go wrong if he followed his actions. After completing the task, Stephen finished in the middle left (heart) to explain how he was successful. Kids can do this independently, with your help, or simply by answering questions with you drawing pictures.

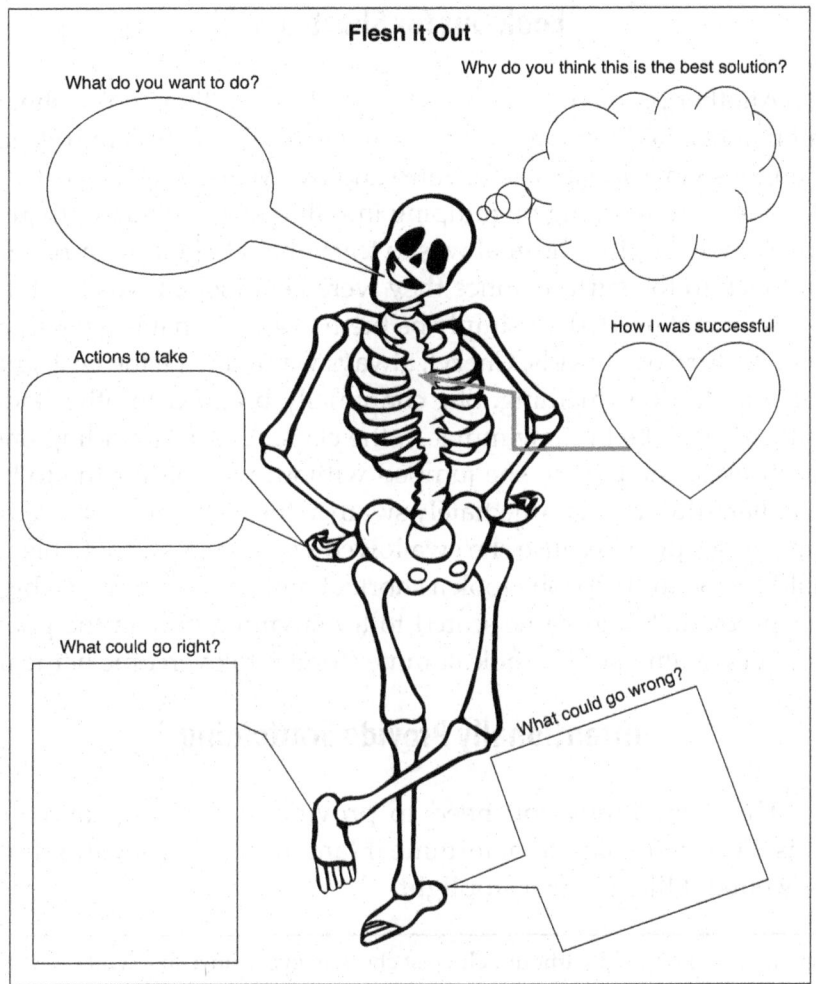

Identify Specific Struggles and Address Them

I mentioned as a part of goal setting that kids can become over-whelmed with a task. For example, a friend asked her son to clean the bathroom. You may have already realized this did not go well. He cleaned at a surface level and forgot to clean the mirror and empty the trash. When I talked with him, he said "It was just too much and I didn't know what to do!" Identify the struggle (clear task for you, vague task for him), and address it by providing a checklist.

Look Out for Shortcuts

Another problem when kids get stuck is that they took a shortcut that resulted in more problems, not less. When I was in college, I taught swimming lessons to four- and five-year-old children. One day, we were working on jumping into the pool, with a depth just above their height. The goal was to teach them to hold their breath and kick to the surface. Since they were beginners, I was there to catch them if needed, or simply be there to grab if that is what they needed. One of my kids, Cheryl, always wanted to be the best, and the first, to do something. She continually bragged to other kids that she was the best swimmer in the class. As I was guiding one kid back to the ladder, she jumped without waiting for me to be near her. Although I immediately swam to the spot, she was coughing and gasping because she swallowed water and was not able to hold on me for help. She took a shortcut and ended up with a bigger problem. She became scared to try anything new in the pool, and it took almost the whole summer for her to overcome her fear.

Intentionally Provide Scaffolding

There are times you need to provide scaffolding for your kids. First, you need to determine if (and how much) scaffolding is needed. I like using a stoplight.

Green	I'm good without help; just check in every once in a while.
Yellow	I'm not real sure what I'm doing; can you help me get started and hang around in case I need you?
Red	I need help. I don't know what to do.

A member of my church adapted this with her first grader. Her daughter chose three stuffed animals, categorized them as described, and they were the symbol. It was common to hear Kaitlyn say, "Mommy, my green alligator is watching me and we are okay," or "Daddy, my yellow bear says I need some help," or "My kitty says we don't know what to do." She explained to me that her friends (stuffed animals) helped her learn.

Next, you need to determine what type of scaffolding is needed. Again, you want to provide help while encouraging autonomy.

Scaffolding Ideas

Use pictures or objects to demonstrate a concept.
Explain using a real-life example.
Ask questions with a forced choice (would you rather fold clothes or vacuum the living room) so that no is not an option.
Give options for kinesthetic learners; use vocabulary cards, blocks for math, or other tools.
Model how you would solve a similar problem.
Use a timer to help kids manage time.
Allow your son or daughter to work in smaller chunks of time, with breaks.

Encourage Preparation to Prevent Problems

One of the most basic ways to help your kids prevent problems is to encourage them to prepare. You'll also need to help with preparation, depending on the age of your kid. There are a variety of ways kids can prepare for a task.

Ways to Prepare for a Task or Activity

♦ Find a quiet place for homework.
♦ Make a list of what to do for chores, activities, or classwork.
♦ Collect any needed materials in advance.
♦ Set a specific time for the task or activity.
♦ If you need help, ask and arrange for that help in a timely manner.
♦ Decide what you need to do about distractions.
   ♦ Some kids need total quiet, so unplugged noise-cancelling headphones can help. Others want background noise, so determine the type of noise and volume in advance. Some need to look at things, such as nature through a window, others need to focus on the task.
   ♦ All kids typically need to turn off their phones.

Nudge in a Positive Manner

Additionally, we need to encourage our kids and nudge them toward progress. We have discussed language in several chapters, but, as a reminder, kids need us to respond to them in positive, not negative ways. They respond to our comments, and we should always focus on words that reassure and inspire them to move forward. Let's look at an example of how a teacher taught his students that making mistakes is a normal part of the learning process.

Robert Brooks and Sam Goldstein share the following:

> One elementary school teacher told her class on the first day of school that throughout the year they would celebrate mistakes. She humorously explained that if her students did not make mistakes, she might lose her job, since it would mean that they already knew everything she had to teach them. She placed a glass jar on her desk with a box of stones and told them, "whenever you or I make a mistake, someone will come up and drop a stone into the jar. As soon as the jar is filled, I will bring in the popcorn for celebration." Apparently the jar was small enough and the stones large enough that the party always took place within the first week. Students who typically would not raise their hands for fear of making a mistake now volunteered to answer; after all, if their answer was incorrect, they would be helping the class move one step closer to celebration.

Teach Them How to Be Self-Controlled

Ultimately, we want our kids to learn and exhibit self-control. Baruch-Feldman, in *Grit for Teens*, provides five strategies that describe ways kids model self-control.

Strategy	Description	What NOT to Do	What to Do
Situation Selection	Choose to be in a situation that ignores impulses and promotes desires	Go to a party where there are drugs	Choose to go to events that are drug-free
Situation Modification	Change the circumstances of the situation to ignore impulses and promote desires	Try to practice singing while TV is on	Turn TV off so you can focus on your singing
Attention Deployment	Focus your attention in ways that avoid temptation or make you more mindful of your choices	Keep phone on and check text messages and social media while trying to do homework	Turn phone off while doing homework
Cognitive Change	Change thinking about the choice to recognize the negatives of impulses and the benefits of long-term goals	Delay homework and are unable to spend time with friends	Think about how finishing your homework so you can enjoy an activity with friends will make you feel
Response Modulation	In the moment, just resist temptation by using willpower and suppressing impulses (least effective method)	Give in to a temper tantrum when you don't get to watch the TV show you want	Next time you and your brother disagree about what to watch, you remember that you are taking turns, so you watch what he wants

Are There Specific Strategies for Students Who Are Stuck in a Personality Type?

We've discussed a wide range of strategies that are effective with most kids. However, there are also four personality types that can impact how kids deal with a failure field: Success-oriented, Overstriver, Failure-avoiding, and Failure-accepting. There are specific strategies that are particularly helpful for each type.

Student Type	Strategies
Success-oriented	Continue to support and encourage their efforts.
Overstriver	Reinforce that effort is just as, or more important than ability, using real-life examples. Positively reinforce the effort they do put forth; deemphasize grades.
Failure-avoiding	Provide opportunities with guaranteed success. Chunk projects so they can complete small steps without being overwhelmed by the big picture. Remind them of past successes, which will build confidence.
Failure-accepting	Provide valid (not too easy so as to be perceived as "dumbed down") opportunities with guaranteed success. Chunk projects so they can complete small steps along with extra support and scaffolding to help them succeed. Consistently reinforce what they are doing right, and praise their efforts.

Summary

+ It's important for your son or daughter not to get stuck in failure mode.
+ Resilience is a life skill and should be nurtured.
+ Share stories of people who have overcome failure, whether they are of characters in stories, people who are famous, members of your community or extended family, or your own.
+ Provide assistance to your kid as he or she attempts to overcome mistakes and failures, but keep an eye on the long-term goal: their independence.

Classroom Connection

Is there something I might ask my kid's teacher(s) about?

+ When my kid gets stuck while learning, how do you help him or her move forward?
+ How can I help my son or daughter develop resilience in terms of academic work?

Are there any ideas I might share with my kid's teacher(s)?

+ Examples of how your kid is resilient in other areas of life.
+ How your son or daughter moves beyond failure in other areas of life or when completing schoolwork at home.

7

Myth Seven

Competition, Grading, and Homework Are No Big Deal

How Should We Handle Competition?

Competition is interwoven into our lives and the lives of our kids. There is competition in sports activities, other activities such as band or chorus, grades, scholarships, colleges, and for adults, jobs, raises, and promotions. Competition is a controversial issue that can generate much debate of the benefits (or lack of) of competition. The research is mixed as to whether competition is good or bad.

Is Competition Good or Bad?

For example, Timothy Gunn, a pediatric neuropsychologist, notes that "Competition helps kids learn that it is not always the best or the brightest who are successful, but rather those that work hard and stick with it. Children who engage in competition earn critical social skills through interacting with other children, while also learning the value of hard work and developing self-esteem and self-efficacy" (www.parents.com/kids/development/social/why-competition-is-good-for-kids-and-how-to-keep-it-that-way/).

Alfie Kohn, in his book *Unconditional Parenting: Moving From Rewards and Punishments to Love and Reason*, takes an opposite view. He points out that "optimal performance at most tasks not only doesn't require people to try to beat one another—it requires that they be freed from such an arrangement. There is no trade-off. Cooperation makes more sense than competition if we care mostly about bottom-line results, just as it does if our prime concern is how people feel about themselves and those around them."

When there is conflicting information, I look for research studies on the topic, and I did so here. I found a study published by the American Psychological Association. The researchers performed a meta-analysis, which means they analyzed studies that had been done on competition and performance to look for patterns. The result of their detailed work? Competition may not be entirely beneficial, but it may not be totally detrimental. In other words, we don't know. It seems that it isn't competition itself that matters, it's a mix of the variables of the type of competition, the motivational aspects of the competition, and even your kid's personality.

Given that information, I'm not going to take a hard stand. My perspective is to accept competition as a part of life and recommend that you strive for your kid to be involved in healthy competition.

Mixed Messages

I know I said it's about doing your best, but . . .
[After losing in competition] Are you sure you did all you could do since you lost?

How Can I Know the Difference Between Healthy and Unhealthy Competition?

If we accept that competition, whether through grades, scholarships, sports, or other activities is a part of our kids' lives, we should turn our attention to the type of competition. There is a clear difference between healthy and unhealthy competition, and we should strive for our kids to be involved in healthy competitive activities.

Characteristics of Healthy and Unhealthy Competition

Healthy Competition	Unhealthy Competition
Kids want to participate	Kids make excuses so they don't have to participate
Kids are excited about the activity	
Kids are learning	Kids are anxious about the activity
Kids feel better about themselves based on the activity	Kids rarely talk about or complain about the activity
	Kids do not seem to be learning anything new
Focus is on the overall performance of the team, while acknowledging individual performance	Kids feel worse about themselves based on the activity
	There is an overemphasis on individual performance
Kids are provided feedback for improvement in a positive manner	There is an overemphasis on competition of members within a team
Intrinsic motivation is nurtured	Kids are provided feedback in a negative manner
Encourages a growth mindset	Kid's intrinsic motivation doesn't matter
Although winning is a part of the goal, so is progress and improvement	Encourages a fixed mindset
	Winning is the focus, to the exclusion of everything else

What Can I Do?

When it comes to competition, the key word is balance. It's certainly fine to encourage your students as they compete, but there is a difference between being encouraging and overbearing. When my nephew played baseball, my sister cheered for him, even if he made a mistake. She was focused on his effort as well as the score of the game. One of the other parents in the crowd was on his feet constantly, yelling at his son, the coaches, and the other players. After the game, my sister thanked the coaches for their work, asked how Matthew could improve, and had a positive conversation with Matthew on the way home. The father who was obsessed with winning and was overly negative in his approach, stormed out of the stands, berated his son for anything less than perfection, and complained about the coaches and other players. If you want to motivate your kid, try the first approach, not the second.

Although we tend to think of sports for competition, there are also competitive aspects of school. As we discussed in Chapter 5, you want to encourage a growth mindset. To do that, deemphasize grades and focus on learning. Whether or not your kid makes the honor roll, celebrate progress. And be careful not to compare your kid's grades to those of your friends' kids.

Finally, be particularly careful of setting up a competition between siblings. Kids naturally compare themselves to their siblings, but we can unintentionally make it worse. I can't tell you the number of parents who said to me "I'm sorry Xavier isn't doing well in your class. His sister is so much smarter than he is." We set our kids up for failure when we measure them against one of their siblings, and it can damage their relationship with their siblings and with us. Annette Breaux, in the following poem, shares how this feels from a kid's perspective. Make sure you are focusing on the unique skills, talents, and personality of each of your kids.

I'm Not My Older Brother

I'm not my older brother
So please do not compare
To treat me as another
Would surely be unfair
He has ways of doing things
Ways that are his own
He's okay, but there's no way
That I'll become his clone
I'm not my older brother
And I do not wish to be
I'm happy to be who I am
And that is simply me.

Annette Breaux
© Annette Breaux. Used with permission.

How Should I Deal With Grading?

Grading is one of the most common issues parents ask me about. We all have memories of grades we received, both good and bad. Despite my age, I remember the B I received in 10th grade economics. I earned an A, but as the teacher wrote on the report card, "Barbara missed a day of class to go on a trip with her father.

Therefore, her grade dropped to a B." I wasn't upset about the B; I didn't like that my grade wasn't based on my work. Grades matter.

There are several purposes of grades. Schools use evaluation to make decisions about placements, particularly in ability-leveled classes or promotion to the next grade level. Grades in high school can determine whether your kid receives a scholarship or which college he or she can attend. Sometimes, grades are used to externally motivate students. Some students respond well to this form of motivation; grades are just a higher-stakes version of receiving a pizza for reading books. You simply can't get away from the fact that grades provide pressure on students. Some thrive in this situation; others suffer. When it comes to grades, we can complicate the situation if we put too much pressure on our kids. Let's look at three key issues related to grading in schools, strategies for effective communication about grades, and how to respond to bad grades.

What Grading Issues Should I Discuss With My Kid's Teacher?

One of the most important actions you can take as a parent is to communicate with your son's or daughter's teacher about grading. Rather than waiting until there is a problem, be proactive and ask your kid's teacher what grades are based upon.

Key Questions to Ask Your Kid's Teacher

How is my kid graded?
How is my kid graded when working in a group?
Can my kid earn extra credit?

How Is My Kid Graded?

First, you need to know the criteria for grades. Does homework count? You might assume so, but I find that it varies from teacher to teacher. Some teachers formally grade homework, others simply provide credit for completion. Certain assigned items may be weighted more heavily than others. One of my university students shared a story that happened to her. Marley was assigned a science project in middle school. She was sick, and freely admitted she didn't do her best work. When she received a low grade, Marley understood, as did her parents. However, when she received her report card, Marley's overall grade was the lowest she had ever received. When they met with her teacher, Marley's parents discovered the project was worth 50% of the total grade. You don't want a surprise like that. Ideally, your kid's teacher has a grading policy which details all the information you need to know. Don't guess if he or she has one. Ask.

How Is My Kid Graded When Working in a Group?

In today's classrooms, there are generally opportunities for students to work in small groups. Oftentimes, that work is graded, which can sometimes take a negative turn. I hated working in a group when I was in school. Because I was very organized, I usually ended up doing most of the work. If someone fell short on their part, I picked up the slack. Our group would earn an A, even if I was the only one who earned it.

This is another conversation to have with your kid's teacher before there is a problem. Start with a general question about how groupwork grades are determined, but you may need to probe for more information.

Questions to Ask About Grading Groupwork

1. How will my son or daughter be graded when he or she works in a group?
2. Will he or she receive an individual grade, group grade, or both?
3. Is he or she graded for the quality of work, the ability to work in a group, or both?
4. What happens if my child has to do someone else's work because he or she isn't completing his or her part?
5. If we (kid or parents) don't agree with a group grade, what can we do?

Mixed Messages

Since you did more work in the group activity at school, I'm going to talk to your teacher about getting a higher grade.
I know you don't like groupwork, especially since the other students pull your grade down.

Can My Kid Earn Extra Credit?

When I was teaching, I struggled with the whole concept of extra credit. It never seemed to accomplish what I thought it would. The students who usually earned it didn't really need it, earning an A plus instead of an A or an A instead of a B. It also seemed to overemphasize points vs. learning. As I work with teachers and parents, I continue to find that extra credit is controversial.

Several years ago, one of my university graduate students was furious because I wouldn't give her extra credit. She was on the borderline between an A and a B, and she wanted me to increase one low grade on a major project because she had done a good job "the rest of the time." In effect, she wanted me to give her extra credit on a very poor assignment because she wanted it.

I considered this request, as well as how a similar situation would conclude in real life. If my husband does extra work on a project for his job, he doesn't get an extra boost in his salary. It may impact his future salary or any raises, but he doesn't get an additional payment for his quality work. On the other hand, if he did a poor job on the project, he certainly doesn't get rewarded for doing something else to make up for it. In other words, extra credit isn't a part of the real world.

I understand that we can all have one bad grade which should not carry too heavy a penalty. But that is a grading issue. I recommend that teachers build a plan with a wide range of assessments, so that one or two low grades does not unnecessarily hurt a student. For me, extra credit doesn't really benefit kids. Grades reflect how much a kid has learned and doing "bonus items" if he or she didn't like his or her grade is not helpful.

Let me add one caveat. Many schools, especially middle and high schools, now use a grading policy called Not Yet Grading or

The Power of I, representing incomplete. Under this type of policy, if students do not complete work at a satisfactory level, they are allowed the opportunity to receive help and redo the work for an improved grade. This is different, as students are given an additional time to master material, and then have a second chance to demonstrate their knowledge. It is usually not applicable for students who have already earned an A and want an A+. I regularly recommend teachers and principals incorporate this as a regular part of grading to help students learn at a higher level.

How Can I Communicate With My Kid's Teacher?

Communicating with your kid's teacher is important for a variety of reasons, but for this chapter, we will focus on connecting about grading. It doesn't matter how you collaborate with your kid's teacher, as long as you do it.

Mixed Messages

I care what your teacher thinks (but you never make time to talk with the teacher).
Nothing your teacher does is right.

Electronic Communication

Most schools provide technology-based options for communicating with your son's or daughter's teacher. At a basic level, you can email the teacher for information, but many teachers post homework on their page on the school website, while some schools provide passwords you can use to access your kid's grades. It's important to find out how the teacher provides grading information, and how you can access it.

Parent-Teacher Conferences

Parent-teacher conferences are one of the most typical ways to communicate with teachers. There may be a conference at the start of the year, but they are usually scheduled to coincide with the release of a report card. I always encourage parents to attend, and to schedule one at a different time if you cannot meet on the school-determined schedule. As I was writing this, a friend asked, "Are you sure I need to go? My son makes all As." Just because your son or daughter has good grades doesn't mean you should skip a conference. Every time you meet with a teacher, it is an opportunity to learn more about your son or daughter and help him or her become even more successful. You can use the sample plan below to shape the direction of your conference.

Parent-Teacher Conference

Goals:	
What Your Kid is Doing Well	What Your Kid is Struggling With
Actions I'll Take as a Teacher to Support Your Kid	Actions You Can Take as a Parent to Support Your Kid

Student-Led Conferences

Some schools now use student-led conferences, which is a type of parent-teacher conference. They have risen in popularity in recent years and they allow students to take a leadership role. Teachers participate, but they move into the role of a facilitator. What does a student-led conference look like?

Structure for Student to Lead Conference

Welcome your guests (family members).
Introduce your teacher.
Share your goals (should be written).
Show your chart that shows progress.
Show examples of your work that is reflected on the chart.
Ask if your guests have any questions.
Ask if your teacher has anything to add.
Complete the summary sheet together.

Your role is to listen to your kid, ask questions, and be proud of their leadership skills.

**Sample Questions to Ask Your Kid During
a Student-Led Conference**

What are you most proud of?
What have you learned?
What are you still working on?
What did you struggle with?
Did you reach your goals?
Questions I have for the teacher as my child presents.

How Should I React to a Bad Grade?

Finally, let's turn our attention to a very specific problem related to grading. What do you do if your kid has a bad grade on his or her report card? This issue was made clear in a letter to the parenting column in the *New York Times*.

My daughter is 12 and in seventh grade. I just found out from her school that they distributed report cards last week and she did not give hers to me. She hid it in a drawer in her room because she didn't want to be grounded for her low grade of 76 in science. She's a really good student and kid for the most part. She has starting the teenager backtalk stuff, but she's over all a really good kid. I have no idea what I should do about her hiding her report card. Should I punish her? Ground her for hiding it? We have an 85 percent rule in the house: her grades need to be 85 percent or above or she is grounded to the house until the next progress report. Advice on what I should do? Alyssa's Mom.
https://parenting.blogs.nytimes.com/2010/11/10/
punishing-a-bad-report-card/

As we discussed in Chapter 1, rewards and punishment typically don't work well in terms of motivating your kid. In this case, Alyssa is afraid, which can lead to dishonesty. I'd suggest that you follow six steps when responding to a bad grade.

How to Respond to a Bad Grade

Don't panic.
Take time to respond.
Ask your kid questions.
Talk to the teacher.
With your kid, set a goal for the future.
Encourage and support your kid.

How Should I Handle Homework?

Homework is a part of most of today's classrooms. Some homework is helpful, some is not. It's the quality of homework not the quantity that makes a difference. Teachers typically assign homework in order to extend learning beyond the classroom. Sometimes they think they don't have enough time to complete everything during class. Other times, they give homework because we believe it teaches responsibility. And, at times, they assign homework because they think parents expect it. The research is mixed as to whether or not homework is beneficial.

Mixed Messages

Homework is important [but you continually allow your kid to do other things].
Homework is important [but you don't provide needed resources].

What does this mean to us? Homework can be helpful, but teachers must plan for its use. Cathy Vatterot, in her book *Rethinking Homework: Best Practices that Support Diverse Needs*, provides some guiding principles that describe effective homework.

Principles for Assigning Homework

Homework should be clearly connected to student learning.

Skills require practice.

More time on task enhances learning.

The quality is as important as the amount of time needed to complete the work.

Children differ in motivation, persistence, and organizational skills and this impacts homework.

Frustration is detrimental to motivation and desire to learn.

What Are the Purposes of Homework?

When you communicate with your kid's teacher, be sure to ask how they use homework.

This can help you communicate with your kids. Cathy suggests sample statements to use with younger and older students.

Sample Statements on the Purpose of Homework

Younger Students	Older Students
The reason for today's homework is . . .	The reason for today's homework is to . . .
◆ so you can practice doing something you learned in school.	◆ allow you to apply something you have already learned to a new situation.
◆ so I can find out if you understand what you learned today.	◆ allow you to pull together several things you have already learned.
◆ to show you something we will learn about soon.	◆ allow you to analyze something you have already learned.

How Can I Help My Kid Get Organized?

One of your most important tasks related to homework is to help your kid get organized. With younger kids, you'll need to structure much of this, and, as they age, you'll shift more responsibility to them. By high school, you should just be checking in at times to make sure everything is moving forward. There are three areas to organize for optimal homework: time, space, and resources.

Time	Space	Resources
When (Scheduling) Length of Time	Where (actual location) Type of space (quiet, computer access, etc.)	Material Resources (computer, paper, textbook, etc.) Human Resources (help from parent for math homework)

What Are Some Other Ways I Can Help My Kid Be Successful With Homework?

Finally, there are some general tips for supporting your son or daughter with his or her homework.

General Tips for Parents

Encourage your son or daughter to give 100% at all times.

Reinforce concepts and habits the teacher is trying to build. If Jonathan is learning how to multiply percents at school, have him help you calculate the tip at a restaurant.

Encourage your son or daughter to set a designated time when homework will be completed every day.

Provide a quiet, well-lit environment at home with all of the materials necessary for completing school tasks (extra paper, scissors, pens, pencils, pencil sharpener, a dictionary, markers, highlighters, a ruler, calculator, index cards, etc.).

Prevent brain freeze—allow your son or daughter to take a short break every 30 minutes or between homework tasks.

Be careful not to give answers to homework questions; instead, offer advice about where to look for an answer.

Model what productive work looks like. When your son or daughter does homework, you do yours too (balance a checkbook, pay the bills, etc.).

Summary

- The research on whether or not competition is beneficial is mixed.
- Look for opportunities for healthy competition and avoid toxic situations.
- Be especially careful that you don't set up situation where your kid feels like he or she is competing with his or her siblings.
- Grading can be high stakes, so be sure you understand what and how your kid's teacher grades.
- Regularly communicate with your son's or daughter's teacher, whether through conferences, phone calls, or electronic options. Don't wait until there is a problem.
- Ask your kid's teacher about the homework policy.
- Support your kid, but don't do the work for him or her.

Classroom Connection

Is there something I might ask my kid's teacher(s) about?

- How do you approach competition in your classroom?
- What is your grading policy? Is there anything specific about your philosophy of grading I should know?
- Are there any tips or strategies that you have found to be particularly effective for homework?

Are there any ideas I might share with my kid's teacher(s)?

- Your concerns and perspective about competition.
- How you plan to emphasize or deemphasize grading; how you would like to communicate with him or her about grading.
- Ideas of what has worked in the past when your kid completes homework and/or any issues with homework.

8

Myth Eight

If I Do Everything Right My Child Will Be Motivated

There are times when nothing you do motivates your son or daughter. It's as if you try your hardest, but things get worse. As we wrap up our discussion, I want to leave you with answers to four key questions.

Four Overall Ideas

What Are the Main Things I Should Remember About My Kids?
What Should I Do When I'm Angry?
What if I Need Help?
Is There Any Other Encouragement You Can Give Me?

What Are the Main Things I Should Remember About My Kids?

Although we have discussed many concepts throughout this book, I want to remind you of several ideas that are helpful when you are feeling helpless.

First, it's not always about them. Sometimes it's the environment, school, friends, siblings, or even you. Second, as the old adage points out, parent the kid you have, not the one you want. Third, check your actions and reactions, because your kids are always watching you. They pay more attention to what you do than to what you say. Next, pick your battles. Sometimes, what is important right now isn't important in the long run. Finally, be careful about second guessing yourself. Although you need to reflect on any changes you need to make, questions like "Were we too soft/hard on them growing up?" or "Will this never end?" usually are not productive.

Mixed Messages

"It's your fault" [even when it is something else].
"I wish you were more like your cousin" [instead of yourself].

What Should I Do When I Am Angry?

One of the times when we feel like we have lost control is when we are angry. I'm never at my best during those times, and I'm guessing you aren't either. Be cautious when you are angry.

Caution When ANGRY

Assess and gather information before saying or doing anything.

Nagging doesn't work; at some point, move on.

Give yourself a time-out. The angrier you are, the more time you need.

React without threats.

Yield to your kid if it's not a battle worth fighting for.

Mixed Messages

"It doesn't matter what you did or didn't do; you lose your phone privileges for a week."

What If I Need Help?

Don't assume you can handle everything on your own. If you need help, ask for it. In addition to speaking with your spouse and any other parents or step-parents, talk to other trusted adults.

> Ask your parents how they handled different issues when
>   you were a kid.
> Ask friends or colleagues how they parent in specific situations.
> Talk with your kid's teacher.
> Speak with a religious advisor, such as a pastor, rabbi, or priest.
> Seek advice from a licensed professional.

Is There Any Other Encouragement You Can Give Me?

Finally, we must consider the X factor: keeping yourself motivated so you can continue to parent. *There is an old saying: you have to take care of yourself before you can take care of others.* When things are not going well, it's important to take time to focus on yourself. Taking care of ourselves means taking time to rest, eating well, getting enough exercise, and having balance in our lives. But it also means being inspired about who we are and what we do. There are seven key ways I incorporate inspiration in my life.

Incorporating Inspiration

1. Build a positive memory file.
2. Read books that inspire.
3. Watch inspirational movies.
4. Find everyday heroes.
5. Surround yourself with motivating thoughts.
6. Keep a success journal.
7. Make the choice every day.

Build a Positive Memory File

You probably have a picture, note or craft item your kid has made. Start today building a memory file with pictures, e-mails, notes, or anything that acknowledges your role as a parent. For example, whenever my husband sees a *Star Wars* figurine, it reminds him of all the times he played with them with his son. If you keep some items, on those days when things get tough, go to your file and look through it. You'll be surprised at how much it will cheer you up. You have these memories in your head; but when you are under a lot of stress, they're hard to remember. Keep these cues handy, so you can be reminded of your impact instantly. What is in your memory file? Where do you keep those tangible memories so you can access them when you need some motivation?

Read Books That Inspire You

I love to read, so I use books to inspire and encourage me. One of my favorites is *The Phantom Tollbooth*, which my father read to me when I was growing up. When I married my husband, his son and I had a good relationship. However, as he grew into a teenager, things became a bit rocky. Whenever something went wrong, I read *The Phantom Tollbooth*. In the book, Milo goes through a magical tollbooth in the Kingdom of Wisdom, which is struggling because the Princesses Rhyme and Reason have been banished. His journey to restore Rhyme and Reason and to become wise always helped me.

Inspiring Books

The Ten Greatest Gifts I Give My Children: Parenting from the Heart by Steven W. Vannoy

The Middle Place by Kelly Corrigan

The Gift of an Ordinary Day: A Mother's Memoir by Katrina Kenison

The Call to Brilliance: A True Story to Inspire Parents and Educators by Ruth Steindel Brown

---

Watch Movies That Inspire You

I also love watching movies about kids and parents to be reminded of the ups and downs of parenting. My favorite movie is an older one: *The Sound of Music*, in which a father learns lessons about his own children from a nun. You probably have your own favorites, but here are some others my friends and I like.

Parenting Movies

Happy Feet

Lorenzo's Oil

Mary Poppins

Mr. Mom

Mrs. Doubtfire

Stepmom

The Pursuit of Happyness

Find Everyday Heroes

When you were growing up, did you have a hero? My nephew loves the Hulk, at least right now. Part of what he likes is that the Hulk is "big and strong and green and he has purple pants; he gets the bad guys." We all need heroes we can admire, especially in a world full of negativity. One of the lessons we learned from September 11, 2001, was that heroes can be normal people who do what they can to help others, such as firefighters and police officers. You can motivate yourself by reminding yourself of the everyday heroes in your life.

My list starts with my father, a coach and a retired university professor who has always taught—his children, his students, and everyone around him. His lessons to me are still powerful: it's important to care about every single student you teach; it's more important to do the right thing than it is to be right all the time. I learned one of his most powerful lessons at a basketball game when I was in high school, and he was the referee. I went with him to a game; and while sitting in the stands, I listened to fans yell at him throughout the entire game. Nothing he did was right, and they called him stupid and some other things that I won't repeat. I was in tears. After the game, he just smiled and said that he never even heard what they said; he just did his job and ignored the rest.

That powerful lesson has stayed with me today in two ways. First, even though I am a rabid college basketball fan, I never yell at the referees. Second, when things get tough, I know I need to do my job and ignore the rest; particularly the unwarranted criticism that can come from those who think they know more about a situation than they do. If I had a dollar for every time someone told me that I couldn't write a book, it was too hard, or someone might not like it, I'd be rich! But none of that was important. I kept my focus, I did my job writing, and I was successful; all the while applying the long-taught lesson from my dad.

Who are your everyday heroes? Is it your spouse? Another family member? Your parents? Friends or neighbors? Make a list, think about them when you are struggling, and seek encouragement from them.

Surround Yourself With Motivating Thoughts

Another important thing I do is create an environment filled with motivating thoughts and pictures. I collect quotes by famous and not-so-famous people on a variety of motivational topics such as persistence, success, and focus. I write some of them in my journal, I put some of them up on a dry erase board in my office, on my computer screen, or anywhere else where I will see them regularly. I've even changed my screen saver so the scrolling text is my quote of the moment; the one that I'm most enamored with each week. I set my background on my computer desktop to be a picture of something that reminds me of what is most important to me. Right now, it's a collage of pictures of my niece and nephew. No matter how crazy it gets at work, I can look at their smiling faces and everything seems a little better. I receive a daily motivation quote by e-mail, which guarantees that no matter how much junk e-mail I get, no matter how many problems people want me to solve, I always get at least one encouraging e-mail per day. I also set my home page to a Web page with motivational thoughts. Again, this forces me at least once, when I log on to the Internet, to see something positive and uplifting.

Inspiring Quotes

"Be the parent today that you want your kids to remember tomorrow."

—Unknown

"Have patience. All things are difficult before they become easy."

—Saadi

"They may forget what you said, but they will never forget how you made them FEEL."

—Carol Buchner

"Don't let yourself become so concerned with raising a good kid that you forget you already have one."

—Glennon Melton-Doyle

"What good mothers and fathers instinctively feel like doing for their babies is usually best after all."

—Benjamin Spock

"So even when it might seem easy to throw in the towel, just hang on. Things are a thousand times brighter on the other side and your children will be better for it."

—Unknown

"Promise me you'll always remember . . . you're braver than you believe, stronger than you seem, smarter than you think, and loved more than you know."

—Christopher Robin (Winnie the Pooh)

Keep a Journal

Journaling is a practice that I still struggle to incorporate in my life, but I have found it to be one of the most critical parts of self-reflection. If the idea of writing pages and pages of daily events doesn't thrill you, don't worry. That's not what I'm talking about. I suggest keeping a list of successes that happen each day, a log of good things that happen. Challenge yourself to write down something positive every day. Even if it's nothing more than that you survived today, write it down. Maybe your son did his chores or your daughter gave you a hug for no reason. Keep the list and keep writing it down. The discipline itself will motivate you and keeping it in a journal allows you to revisit it on the stressful days.

Make the Choice—Every Day

Ultimately, motivating yourself is about making a choice every single day that you are going to do your best, and you are going to stay positive—no matter what. It may be just remembering that you do make a difference. Or it may be continuing to be a great parent; even when your kid is yelling at you. It is getting up every day to start again, even when you don't see that you are making a difference. It's believing the best, even when your kids don't act their best. One thing that great parents have in common is that they keep themselves motivated and they do whatever it takes to make that happen.

The X factor is giving yourself a daily dose of motivation. Make the commitment now to starting every day off RIGHT!

Remind yourself of why you are a parent and what you like about parenting.

Invest energy in positive activities, alone, with family or friends, and with your kids.

Grin—it's contagious.

Hang out with positive people when you need a break from your kids.

Take time to reflect and renew.

Summary

- Remember there are a variety of factors that impact your kid's motivation.
- When you are frustrated and angry, take a deep breath before you act.
- Don't hesitate to ask for help or advice; other perspectives can be beneficial.
- No matter what, take care of yourself. When you do, you will be a better parent.

Classroom Connection

Is there something I might ask my kid's teacher(s) about?

- How do you keep yourself motivated when you have a tough day?
- Would you tell me three positive things about my son or daughter?
- Can you give me advice about (the challenge you are facing).

Are there any ideas I might share with my kid's teacher(s)?

- How the struggles you have with your kid are impacting school.
- The importance of taking care of yourself.
- How you keep yourself motivated.

Works Cited and Suggested Readings

Bain, K. (2012). *What the best college students do*. Cambridge, MA: The Belknap Press of Harvard University Press.

Baruch-Feldman, C. (2017). *The grit guide for teens: A workbook to help you build perseverance, self-control & a growth mindset*. Oakland: Instant Help Books.

Blackburn, B. R. (2005). *Classroom motivation from A to Z: How to engage your students in learning*. New York: Routledge.

Blackburn, B. R. (2008). *Literacy from A to Z: Engaging students in reading, writing, speaking, & listening*. New York: Routledge.

Blackburn, B. R. (2012). *Rigor made easy*. New York: Routledge.

Blackburn, B. R. (2014). *Rigor in your classroom: A toolkit for teachers*. New York: Routledge.

Blackburn, B. R. (2016a). *Classroom instruction from A to Z: How to promote student learning* (2nd ed.). New York: Routledge.

Blackburn, B. R. (2016b). *Motivating struggling learners: Ten strategies for student success*. New York: Routledge.

Blackburn, B. R. (2017). *Rigor and assessment in the classroom*. New York: Routledge.

Blackburn, B. R. (2018). *Rigor is not a four-letter word* (3rd ed.). New York: Routledge.

Breaux, A. (2004). *The poetry of Annette Breaux*. New York: Eye on Education.

Brooks, R. and Goldstein, S. (2001). *Raising resilient children*. New York: McGraw – Hill.

Campbell, K. and Kahler, K. (2012). *Confident kids: How parents can raise positive, confident, resilient and focused kids*. San Bernardino: Authors.

Canter, L. and Canter, M. (1994). *What to do when your child hates to read: Motivating the reluctant reader*. Santa Monica: Canter & Associates.

Canter, L. and Hausner, L. (1987). *Homework without tears: A parent's guide for motivating children to do homework and to succeed in school*. New York: Harper & Row.

Capuano, D. (2012). *Motivate your son: Inspire your boy to be engaged in school, excited for college, and energized for success.* Old Saybrook: Student Mastery Publishing.

Daniels, L. (2016). *Grit for kids: 16 top steps for developing grit, passion, willpower, and perseverance in kids for self-confidence and a successful life.* Columbia, SC: Author.

Deckers, L. (2016). *Motivation: Biological, psychological, and environmental* (4th ed.). New York: Routledge.

DiBernardo, M. (2015). *8 keys to unlocking your child's potential & development in sports & beyond: There is a formula for success.* San Bernardino: Author.

Dixon, E. (2013). *Helping boys learn: 6 secrets for your son's success in school.* San Bernardino: Author.

Duckworth, A. L. and Gross, J. J. (2014). Self-control and grit: Related but separable determinants of success. *Current Directions in Psychological Science.* 23(5). 319–325.

Faber, A. and Mazlish, E. (2012). *How to talk so kids will listen & listen so kids will talk* (updated ed.). New York: Scribner.

Ferlazzo, L. (2013). *Self-driven learning: Teaching strategies for student motivation.* New York: Routledge.

Fuller, C. (1990). *Motivating your kids from crayons to career: How to enhance your child's learning and achievement without pressure.* Tulsa: Honor Books.

Ginsberg, K. R. and Jablow, M. (2011). *Building resilience in children and teens: Giving kids roots and wings* (2nd ed.). Elk Grove Villave, IL: American Academy of Pediatrics.

Harris, B. (2008). *Confident parents, remarkable kids: 8 principles for raising kids you'll love to live with.* Avon, MA: Adams Media.

Hart, S. and Hodson, V. (2006). *Respectful parents, respectful kids: 7 keys to turn family conflict into co-operation.* Encinitas: Puddle Dancer Press.

Hartley-Brewer, E. (1998). *Motivating your child: Tools and tactics to help your child be a self-starter.* London: Vermilion.

Hoerr, T. R. (2013). *Fostering grit.* Alexandria, VA: Association of Supervision and Curriculum Development.

Hudley, C. and Gottfried, A. (2008). *Academic motivation and the culture of school in childhood and adolescence.* New York: Oxford University Press.

Kohn, A. (1993). *Punished by rewards: The trouble with gold stars, incentive plans, A's, praise, and other bribes.* New York: Houghton Mifflin.

Kohn, A. (2005). *Unconditional parenting: Moving from rewards and punishments to love and reason.* New York: Atria Paperback.

Kurcinka, M. (2001). *Kids, parents, and power struggles: Winning for a lifetime.* New York: William Morrow Paperbacks.

Kurcinka, M. (2015). *Raising your spirited child* (3rd ed.). New York: William Morrow Paperbacks.

Lane, N. (2010). *A better way: 101 practical ways to motivate your child.* San Bernardino: The Lane Connection.

Lewis, K. (2018). *The good news about bad behavior: Why kids are less disciplined than ever-and what to do about it.* New York: PublicAffairs.

Marzano, R. J., Pickering, D. J. and Pollock, J. E. (2001). *Classroom instruction that works.* Alexandria, VA: Association for Supervision and Curriculum Development.

Maslow, A. (1943). A theory of human motivation. *Psychological Review.* 50. 370–396.

Miller, A. (2015). *Freedom to fail: How do I foster risk-taking and innovation in my classroom?* Alexandria, VA: ASCD.

Morin, A. (2017). *13 things mentally strong parents don't do: Raising self-assured children and training their brains for a life of happiness, meaning, and success.* New York: William Morrow Paperbacks.

Murayama, K. and Elliot, A. J. (2012). The competition-performance relation: A meta-analytic review and test of the opposing processes model of competition and performance. *Psychological Bulletin.* 138. 1035–1070. doi:10.1037/a0028324.

Pearlman, C. (2017). *Ignore it!: How selectively looking the other way can decrease behavioral problems and increase parental satisfaction.* New York: TarcherPerigree.

Phelan, T. (2016). *1–2–3 magic: 3-step discipline for calm, effective, and happy parenting* (6th ed.). Naperville: Sourcebooks, Inc.

Pink, D. H. (2011). *Drive: The surprising truth about what motivates us.* New York: Riverhead Books.

Reeve, J. (2014). *Understanding motivation and emotion* (6th ed.). Hoboken: Wiley.

Ricci, M. and Lee, M. (2016). *Mindsets for parents: Strategies to encourage growth mindsets in kids*. Waco, TX: Prufrock Press Inc.

Ryan, R. and Deci, E. (2017). *Self-determination theory: Basic psychological needs in motivation, development, and wellness*. New York: The Guilford Press.

Sandberg, S. and Grant, A. (2017). *Option b: Facing adversity, building resilience, and finding joy*. New York: Knopf.

Sanguras, L. (2017). *Grit in the classroom: Building perseverance for excellence in today's students*. Waco, TX: Prufrock Press Inc.

Silver, D. and Stafford, D. (2017). *Teaching kids to thrive: Essential skills for success*. Thousand Oaks: Corwin.

Simmons, R. (2018). *Enough as she is: How to help girls move beyond impossible standards of success to live healthy, happy, and fulfilling lives*. New York: HarperCollins Publishers.

Stixrud, W. and Johnson, N. (2018). *The self-driven child: The science and sense of giving your kids more control over their lives*. New York: Viking.

Tate, M. (2011). *Preparing children for success in school and life: 20 ways to increase your child's brain power*. Thousand Oaks: Corwin.

Tobias, C. (2012). *You can't make me (but I can be persuaded)* (revised and updated ed.). Colorado Springs: Waterbrook Press.

Whitley, M. (2001). *Bright minds, poor grades: Understanding and motivating your underachieving child*. New York: TarcherPerigree.

Wilson, R. and Lyons, L. (2013). *Anxious kids anxious parents: 7 ways to stop the worry cycle and raise courageous & independent children*. Deerfield Beach: Health Communications, Inc.